# Fathers and Children Together

Full of research-backed advice, examples, and reflection questions throughout, this book is for fathers seeking to build their parenting identity while effectively supporting their child from conception to adulthood.

Covering topics such as opportunities for fathers to connect to their children during each stage of development, occasions for men to grow and develop when they become fathers, advice for healthy and successful coparenting, as well as how to support a positive father-child relationship, this book provides important answers to questions that fathers frequently ask about parenting.

*Fathers and Children Together* is a must read for fathers aspiring to create strong connections to their children, as well as all parents, practitioners, and students in disciplines such as psychology, human development and family studies, parent education, and social work.

**Jay Fagan** is Professor Emeritus in the School of Social Work at Temple University, Philadelphia, PA, and former Co-director of the Fatherhood Research and Practice Network. He was the founding editor of the journal *Fathering*. He taught human behavior and social environment courses at Temple University for 31 years.

**Glen Palm** is a Professor Emeritus of Child and Family Studies at St. Cloud State University, St. Cloud, MN, where he taught Child Development, Family Studies, and Parent Education. He has practiced parent education with fathers in a variety of settings (education, health care and corrections) for more than 40 years.

# Fathers and Children Together

## A Guide to Developing a Parenting Identity and Supporting Your Child

Jay Fagan and Glen Palm

Routledge
Taylor & Francis Group

NEW YORK AND LONDON

Designed cover image: © Getty Images

First published 2024
by Routledge
605 Third Avenue, New York, NY 10158

and by Routledge
4 Park Square, Milton Park, Abingdon, Oxon, OX14 4RN

*Routledge is an imprint of the Taylor & Francis Group, an informa business*

ISBN: 978-1-032-77959-1 (pbk)
ISBN: 978-1-003-48610-7 (ebk)

DOI: 10.4324/9781003486107

Typeset in Palatino
by Deanta Global Publishing Services, Chennai, India

# Dedication

Jay dedicates this book to his wife, Jo; two daughters, Anna Fried and Lisa Fagan; and his grandchildren, Jordan and Norah Fried.

Glen dedicates this book to his wife, Jane Ellison; children, Marisha, Noah, and Allison; and his grandchildren, Hugo Palm and Olympia and Hosea Palm-Husby.

# Contents

# Preface

We (Jay and Glen) wrote this book because we believed that fathers, mothers, practitioners, students, and others deserve to know more about the growing body of information about fathers, as well as how that information translates into practical strategies for raising children. We have each spent more than 30 years studying and working with fathers. We have learned that men desire to learn more about being a father and they often do not know where to turn for reliable information. They want to know how children develop from before birth until adulthood and how their parenting will need to change during each stage of development. They want to know more about how to be a good father and to connect with their children. They want to know how to handle the day-to-day stresses of parenting and work and how they can grow and develop as their children mature. This book addresses these questions and concerns.

Many fathers are reluctant to seek out books about parenting or child development because they are written for women and mothers. This book speaks directly to fathers. Our in-depth review of fathering research at each stage of child development will be of interest to men who want to know what science says about effective fathering. The rapidly growing knowledge about men's parenting is seldom translated for non-researchers. A search on Amazon for books on fathers yielded 81 published advice books on how to be a better father, excluding "dad joke books." The books were authored by celebrities, practitioners, fathers, and clergy. We believe that readers deserve more than a simplified advice book about positive parenting. We are aware of only one book that focuses on translating scientific research about fathers (*Do Fathers Matter? What Science is Telling Us About the Parent We Overlooked* by Paul Raeburn). Raeburn's book uses research to share insights into our understanding of fathers but is based on interviews with researchers. We have spent our entire careers conducting original research and working directly with fathers and believe our experience uniquely qualifies us to write this book.

This book is innovative in that we address the major developmental tasks throughout each stage of childhood. We review the important research findings on fathers' contributions and challenges to supporting their child's growth and development. Although there are a number of excellent book-length reviews of fathering during each stage of child development, these reviews are written for researchers, with technical writing style and often extensive information on the methods used to conduct individual studies. Our book is written in a conversational style, which is more accessible to nonresearchers. We summarize the research findings and their implications for fathers' parenting practices and avoid discussions about research methods.

This book is more than just a review of research on fathers and child development. Each chapter of the book offers opportunities for fathers to reflect on the important values to pass on to children and how these can guide parenting practices. Reflecting on their values helps fathers to be more thoughtful, intentional, understanding, and consistent in parenting. Fathers may want to engage in self-reflection when they read the reflection questions or they may want to discuss the questions with their wives or partners.

Fathers' own growth and development is a major theme throughout the book. The title indicates that the book is a guide to developing a parenting identity. Becoming a father is one of the most demanding periods of growth and development for men. Building this new identity as a father includes deciding what kind of father they want to become and how their role as father fits with their other roles (husband, partner, provider, friend). The integration of these social roles into a new identity is a demanding developmental task. Fathers are challenged to grow and adapt as their children grow and develop. Building an identity as a father is an ongoing process that does not stop once a baby is born but continues throughout a child's growth and development and into the child's adulthood.

You can approach this book in several ways. You may want to read the entire book at once or read the chapters of the book that are relevant to the age of your child(ren). We review theories and concepts introduced in earlier chapters so that you will not feel lost picking up the book in any later chapter. We do suggest that you read Chapter 1, even if you skip around in the other chapters. Keep in mind, however, that if you pick up the book years from now as your child moves to the next stage that there will be new research about fathers to consider.

We wrote this book for fathers. But mothers, practitioners, and students in disciplines such as psychology, human development and family studies, parent education, and social work will find the book useful. We have observed over many years that mothers are interested in knowing more about how fathers experience the parenting role. They want to know about men's development as fathers and they want to know how fathers influence child development. We hope that mothers find this book useful. Human service practitioners may also find this book helpful because they inevitably work with fathers or with clients who bring up issues regarding fathers. Further, most graduate school programs in human services and education offer little or no content about fathers in their curricula. We hope this book can serve as a source of continued education to these professionals. Also, many human service professionals and educators are parents, too, so this book can serve a double purpose as a source of continued education as well as a book to enhance personal parenting practices.

Glen will share insights from parent education classes with fathers that he has facilitated since 1978 in the book. Jay has conducted evaluations of parent education and support programs for fathers. Parent education classes can be a great way for men to learn more about children and parenting practices. Parent education classes come in a variety of formats. In Glen's experience the most effective parenting education is a rich blend of information, reflection, discussion, and social support. There are transition times in children's development and family life where parent education classes can guide and support fathers as they face new challenges. We believe that parent education can be an important supplement to the information in our book. While programs for fathers are offered in many different settings from health care to education to correctional facilities, we advocate for more opportunities for fathers to have access to this resource.

Raising and caring for children is the most significant role that a man can occupy. A great deal has been learned about fathers and children during the past several decades. We hope this book affirms the importance of involved fathers to guide children's development and to build stable family systems and healthy communities.

# Acknowledgments

The authors would like to acknowledge our Routledge editor, Rebecca Collazo, for her support of this project. We would also like to acknowledge Lisa Bolin Hawkins for the help she provided in copyediting the book. She helped us to make the book more readable for fathers. We are exceedingly grateful for her contribution. We acknowledge the comments on an early draft of the book from Deborah Campbell and Paul Wenner that helped to clarify the format and style of the book. We also appreciate the comments from fathers that were shared at the beginning of chapters. Glen acknowledges the many fathers that have been in parent groups that he has facilitated and the collective knowledge about fathers and parenting that have been shared through these experiences. It has been enlightening to see the changes in fathers' attitudes and behavior during the generations from the late 1970s until the present time.

# About the Authors

Jay Fagan, Ph.D., is Professor Emeritus in the School of Social Work at Temple University, Philadelphia, PA, and former codirector of the Fatherhood Research and Practice Network. His research has focused on father–child relationships and coparenting in non-residential and low-income families; responsible fatherhood programs; coparenting interventions for low-income mothers and fathers; fathers with children in Head Start and child welfare; and adolescent fathers. He published the textbooks *New Research on Parenting Programs for Low-income Fathers* (Routledge, 2021), with Dr. Jessica Pearson; *Fathers and Early Childhood Programs* (Cengage Learning, 2004), with Dr. Glen Palm; and *Clinical and Educational Interventions with Fathers* (Routledge, 2001), with Dr. Alan J. Hawkins. Jay has published 100 peer-reviewed research papers, mostly on fathers. He was the founding editor of the journal *Fathering*. He taught human behavior and social environment courses at Temple University.

Glen Palm, Ph.D., is Professor Emeritus of Child and Family Studies at St. Cloud State University, St. Cloud, MN, where he created and coordinated the Parent Education Licensure Program. Glen worked as a parent educator in Early Childhood Family Education (ECFE) programs in Minneapolis and St. Cloud for over 40 years. He started the Dad's Project in St. Cloud which piloted a variety of programs for fathers and families with young children. Glen has written extensively about fathers, ethics, and parent education including co-authoring four books: *Working with Fathers: Methods & Perspectives* (Nu Ink, 1992), *Group Parent Education* (SAGE Publications, 2004), *Fathers and Early Childhood Programs* (Cengage Learning, 2004), and *Parent Education: Working with Groups and Individuals* (Cognella Academic Publishing, 2018).

# Changing Role of Fathers

## Diverse Contexts, Experiences, and Opportunities

*The guys who fear becoming fathers don't understand that fathering is not something perfect men do, but something that perfects men.[1]*

—*Frank S. Pittman*

## Introduction

Today's fathers have redefined what it means to be a dad. The image of fathers as breadwinners and disciplinarians who seldom engaged in caregiving has given way to new expectations. Modern-day fathers are expected to be nurturers, child-centric, engaged, and equal partners with mothers in the care of children while continuing to be providers or coproviders. Fathers encounter many challenges in meeting these expectations. They face pressures to be good providers, to balance work and parenting, and often to be loving husbands and life partners. They face additional pressures from employers who expect them to be available by email or cell phone at all hours and to work seven days per week. Some fathers may be doing all this as unmarried coparents, living separately from their children. The pressures to be a good dad can cause anxiety and stress, as suggested by Frank Pittman in the beginning of this chapter, when expectations are

DOI: 10.4324/9781003486107-1

high and preparation and support are limited. Men often lack role models to guide their quest to be involved and nurturant fathers. They lack knowledge about how to care for and raise healthy, well-adjusted children. They have limited supports to turn to when they need advice about parenting.

We write this book for fathers who aspire to have strong emotional connections to their children. There are many sources on how to be a nurturant father, but this book differs from most popular literature because we rely on research and the authors' practice experiences to write about fathers. The authors have each spent more than 30 years conducting research and working directly with fathers. We will translate the research and our experience in accessible, meaningful ways.

This book will answer questions that fathers frequently ask about parenting, such as:

◆ What are the most important tasks that children should typically accomplish during each stage of development?

◆ What is the father's role in helping children to achieve these tasks?

◆ What opportunities help fathers to connect to their children during each stage to support a positive father–child relationship?

◆ In what ways do men grow and develop as persons when they become fathers?

◆ What does it mean to coparent with the child's mother and why is healthy coparenting essential for raising well-adjusted children?

The book will also pose questions to fathers for their personal reflection as they build their own parenting identity, such as:

◆ What values do you want to teach your child?

◆ How will these values prepare your children for the uncertain future they will face?

◆ How might you want to parent differently from your own fathers/parents?

## Understanding Child Development

The growth and development of the child guides our discussion of fatherhood in this book. "Development" refers to the changes we go through as we get older. Child development has been a central component of Glen's parent education work and Jay's research work with fathers. There are many ways that understanding child development can be useful to fathers: It helps fathers to know what is typical and informs and tempers their expectations. It can also encourage fathers to be involved and affirm their importance to their child's growth and development.

There are many ways to understand children's development, but our discussion is based on the ecological-systems perspective. This perspective suggests that children's lives are embedded in networks of systems that influence all aspects of their development. These systems include a child's everyday interactions (e.g., family, schools), those that are less direct (neighborhood), and those that are even more removed yet still important. Fathers are one component of the child's environment. (We describe the ecological systems perspective in greater detail later in this chapter.)

This book is organized by the stages of child development. There is a chapter on becoming a father before the child's birth, the transition to parenthood, fathers and infants and toddlers, fathers and preschoolers, fathers and school-age children, fathers and adolescents, and fathers and young adult children. We focus on each developmental stage because parents must adjust their parenting practices as their children mature and grow.

For many years, researchers have largely neglected to include fathers in their studies of children. In contrast, we have been involved in and have observed the increasing interest in understanding fathers and their influence on children over the past three decades. We believe this book will help readers understand and appreciate the essential role fathers play in the development and well-being of children.

## Guiding Principles

Six principles guide our discussions about fathers and children throughout the book:

Principle 1: While there are significant differences between the ways in which fathers and mothers engage with children, there are also many similarities. The essential tasks of parenting are the same for fathers and mothers.[2] There is no parenting behavior that is completely unique to fathers.

Principle 2: Fathers must grow and adapt as children grow and develop. A parent's behavior affects their child's development and children also impact their parent's development. Fathers must also adapt to the many changes that families encounter, such as the death of a family member, employment transitions, natural disasters, and public health crises.

Principle 3: Any discussion about fathers must consider the context of fathers' lives. Context may include the quality of the father's relationship with his wife or partner, the father's work environment, the family neighborhood/housing situation, and whether the father lives with his child or not. A father's gender orientation, marital status, and educational and family backgrounds are also part of the context.

Principle 4: Fathers' beliefs about masculinity and gender influence their beliefs about how to raise children, what they think their role should be, and how they interact with their children and their partners. Fathers' beliefs about masculinity are influenced by a society's dominant gender ideologies, which are the beliefs about the importance of adhering to culturally defined standards for gendered behavior. Ideas of masculinity in the United States, Canada, and many European countries tend to be diverse. Some men are exposed to traditional masculinity ideologies, which state that men should never show weakness, should not be feminine, should strive for success in the workplace, and should take risks. J. Randles has suggested that many men adhere to a "hybrid" type of masculinity,[3] which suggests that men should be highly involved and nurturant with children, expressive with feelings, and egalitarian in dealings with women. Despite these changes, traditional gender ideas—viewing fathers as discretionary and secondary helpers whose primary responsibility is breadwinning—are still around.[4]

**Principle 5:** Expectations of fathers and fathers' expectations of themselves are influenced by culture, race, and ethnicity. Although there is a growing trend across most parts of the world for fathers to be actively involved in caregiving, there are nonetheless significant differences in the ways in which fathers are involved with children. For example, when asked about the role that fathers play in their children's lives, Chinese fathers emphasize their role as educators, whereas fathers in the United States emphasize their role as nurturers and role models. Expectations for fathers are greatly influenced by how fathers are portrayed on social media. For example, African American fathers have been portrayed in the media as uninvolved and disengaged from their children even though researchers have demonstrated that Black fathers are as involved, and sometimes more involved, with children than fathers in other ethnic groups.[5]

**Principle 6:** Fathers need to consider their own values and decide what they want to pass on to their children. This will influence all their decisions about how to raise children. Fathers' values may include beliefs about children's obedience to authority, children's religious education and participation, how children should dress, extracurricular activities (e.g., sports, arts activities), and much more. Children learn how to act by watching their fathers and mothers—they imitate their parents and the values that are important to them. "Reflective parenting" is a related concept that focuses on understanding a child's thinking, feelings, and intentions.[6] We strive to support fathers' reflective capacity to consider children's and their own thoughts, feelings, and intentions during each stage of child development. We will provide reflective questions throughout the book to support this skill.

## Defining Terms

Researchers and practitioners use several terms when writing or talking about fathers. For example, the terms *fatherhood* and *fathering* do not mean the same thing.

*Fatherhood* refers to fertility status or paternity, with *paternity* being biological fatherhood. Fatherhood can also be achieved through legal adoption of a child.

In contrast, *fathering* describes the behaviors and identity aspects of being a father.[7] A father who has conceived or adopted a child may never be actively involved or may be highly involved in his child's life. The extent and nature of his involvement make up his fathering behavior, also sometimes called *father involvement*. We use the terms *father involvement* and *fathering* interchangeably in this book.

Another term that is sometimes used is *social father*, that is, men who assume responsibility for raising children when they may or may not be biological or adoptive fathers. *Social fathers* can include uncles, grandfathers, other kin, or non-relatives who are in the role of father.

Four important questions about fathers make up the rest of this chapter: (1) What is meant by "father involvement"? (2) How has the father's role changed in the latter part of the twentieth and beginning of the twenty-first century? (3) Why are some fathers more involved with children than other fathers? (4) How do diverse contexts influence fathering in the United States?

## Father Involvement

Before the 1980s, there were very few studies that included fathers and there was no consistent idea of father involvement. The researchers Michael Lamb and Joseph Pleck made the first major attempt to describe father involvement, suggesting a broad definition that included fathers' accessibility, engagement, and responsibility for children.[8] They defined "accessibility" as the time the father is available to the child, whether or not he is interacting directly with the child. "Engagement" referred to father–child shared interactions, such as playing together, hugging, or putting the child to bed. "Responsibility" referred to a father organizing and planning activities and providing resources to a child. For example, making a doctor's appointment for a child is an organizing activity. This model was an important development because it drew attention to the different kinds and quantities of father involvement associated with caring for and socializing children.[9] Many researchers and practitioners adopted this framework.

In recent years, however, researchers and practitioners have recognized limitations with these ideas of father involvement. They now emphasize the quality, in addition to quantity, of fathers' involvement with children because quality of involvement is central to positive child development. Measures of quality may include acceptance of the child, closeness, conflict, emotional support, nurturance, responsiveness, and warmth.

## Changing Role of Fathers

After World War II, during the 1950s and 1960s, most mothers in middle- and higher-income families stayed home to care for children while fathers worked outside of the home. Mothers changed diapers, fed children, helped with homework, provided emotional support, planned children's play dates, and much more. Fathers usually engaged in these activities more as helpers than as equal coparents. Nonetheless, some fathers were highly involved in these types of activities with their children, particularly low-income fathers, whose families, needed the income of two parents to provide for basic needs and to avoid poverty. Care for children in low-income families was often provided by a combination of fathers, mothers, grandparents, aunts and uncles, and older siblings.

The role of fathers started to change about 50 years ago, sometime between the 1970s and 1980s. Researchers observed that the culture of fatherhood was changing.[10] The role of fathers was no longer considered only breadwinner and disciplinarian, but now also involved greater emotional involvement, nurturing, and caregiving. There were many reasons for these changes. Women entered the labor force in large numbers at that time and consequently were less available to provide all the direct care to children, so fathers were needed to take on some of the childcare. Further, the women's movement had a substantial influence on attitudes about the roles of men and women in families. Also, the supply of licensed childcare programs expanded in the 1980s and 1990s, providing parents with alternative options for childcare.[11]

Family researchers have closely studied these changes in fathers' and mothers' behaviors and attitudes about parenting and family life. Sociologist Ralph LaRossa has written that the shift was more in cultural attitudes and expectations than it was in actual fathering behavior.[12] Fathers and those around them expected fathers to be equal parenting partners with mothers, but equal sharing in the care of children rarely occurred.

One way to look at the changing role of fathers is to compare how much time men spend with children today compared with prior years. The best source of information regarding time spent with children comes from the American Time Use Study and the earlier Americans' Use of Time Study,[13] which indicate that fathers who lived in the same household with children doubled the amount of time they spent with children between 1985 and 2019.

Text Box 1.1 shows the overall amount of time mothers and fathers spent taking care of children in 2019—caring for children's physical needs (e.g., bathing young children), reading to children, playing with them, and engaging in activities related to children's education. Mothers with children ages 0–5 and 6–12 spent more total time caring for children. The largest discrepancy between fathers and mothers was in the provision of physical care to children ages 6–12: Mothers spent almost three times as much time providing physical care to children in this age group compared with fathers. The amount of time playing with children was about equal in the 0–5 and 6–12 age groups. Fathers spent slightly more time playing with 6–12-year-olds compared to mothers. These statistics are pre-Covid and likely do not accurately reflect the amount of time fathers and mothers spent with children during the height of the pandemic.

**TEXT BOX 1.1**

Average hours per day parents spent caring for and helping children in their household as their main activity, 2019 annual averages.

| Activity | Fathers, child under age 18 | Mothers, child under age 18 | Fathers, youngest child 6–12 | Mothers, youngest child 6–12 | Fathers, child under age 6 | Mothers, child under age 6 |
|---|---|---|---|---|---|---|
| Total, caring for and helping children | .91 | 1.74 | .65 | 1.17 | 1.42 | 2.75 |
| Physical care for children | .28 | .69 | .12 | .33 | .51 | 1.25 |
| Reading to and with children | .03 | .06 | .02 | .04 | .06 | .10 |
| Playing with children, not sports | .30 | .36 | .12 | .11 | .56 | .71 |
| Activities related to children's education | .06 | .15 | .09 | .14 | .05 | .17 |

Source: U.S. Bureau of Labor Statistics (2022), *American time use survey summary.*

One could conclude from these data that because fathers spent more time in childcare in 2019 than they did 1985, mothers must be doing less. This would make sense, because paid work has taken up a larger share of women's overall time since the mid-1980s. But the picture is more complicated—fathers spent more time in childcare, but so did mothers. This trend has been called the "ideology of intensive mothering." This phrase was coined in 1996 by researcher Sharon Hayes, who argued that modern-day mothers strive to maximize their children's development by engaging in "child-centered, expert-guided, emotionally absorbing, labor intensive, and financially expensive parenting".[14] The ideology of intensive mothering was a phenomenon that first occurred among college-educated women. Today, intensive mothering is shared by almost all mothers, regardless of education level. Between 2003 and 2017, time spent among mothers with a college degree or higher stalled.[15] Time spent among mothers with a high school degree or less continuously increased.

Fathers' attitudes about parenthood have changed along with their increasing time spent in fathering. One of the authors of this book (Glen) found that most of the men in the groups that he has worked with want to be actively involved and have close, warm relationships with their children. A study of 932 male partners of women who participated in the National Survey of Fertility Barriers (a United States study) showed that most fathers and non-fathers want to have children.[16] Fewer than 10% of fathers in that study indicated that becoming a father was not important to them. These attitude changes are sometimes referred to as the "new fatherhood ideal." But fathers also embrace the traditional role of men as the main financial provider in the family.[17] Men place a high value on fatherhood, but they also place a high value on work. James Levine's book on working fathers highlights this work–family tension for men as well as women and offers strategies for balancing work and family life for fathers.[18]

Several additional trends illustrate how fathers' roles have changed. More fathers stay at home to care for their children while mothers work. There has been an increase in the number of divorced fathers who have joint custody of children, combining legal and physical custody. (The two types of custody arrangements in the United States are legal custody, which refers to parents' shared decision making for children, and physical custody, which refers to parents' coresiding with the child.) The increase in the number of fathers who have joint custody has largely resulted from the trend for states to adopt joint legal and physical custody options in divorce proceedings. These changes have significant effects on fathers' direct involvement with children.[19]

The research on fathers' and mothers' parenting behavior and attitudes can be confusing when one is trying to determine the extent to which the role of fathers has changed. Liana Sayer's study of these issues helps to lessen the confusion.[20] She and her colleagues focused on the ratio of mothers' to fathers' involvement in childcare. They found that the ratio of mothers' to fathers' *developmental childcare* (e.g., playing, reading, helping with education activities) did not change much from 1985 to 2012, but the ratio of mothers' to fathers' *physical childcare* (e.g., feeding, dressing, putting to bed) decreased substantially over this period. This is largely because both fathers and mothers doubled their time in developmental childcare. Fathers' and mothers' physical childcare time increased during this time, but mothers' physical childcare time increased at a much slower rate than fathers' physical childcare time. These findings provide the most significant evidence that fathers are assuming a more important role in parenting than they did in past decades.

## Why Some Fathers Are More Involved Than Others

### Economic and Sociological Theories

There is no one theory or explanation for why some fathers are more involved or engaged with children than other fathers. Sociologists, psychologists, and economists have developed theories based on their own studies, and as one would expect, they focus on different aspects of human behavior, interaction, and social organization. Economists suggest that people make rational choices about different types of family work, including who takes care of children's needs. The essence of this theory is that individuals in families make choices based on who is more efficient at tasks. Parents specialize in different tasks to meet the needs of the family. Parents' work inside and outside the home is very time-consuming, and because time is limited, fathers and mothers must decide who is most efficient at each task. Often fathers have higher earnings than mothers, either because the workplace discriminates against women or because women reduce or stop work to care for children. This theory suggests that fathers will specialize in work outside the home when they have higher earnings than mothers. However, economists have acknowledged that specialization does not completely explain fathers' and mothers' roles in the family. Parents have many reasons other than relative incomes for making rational choices about who does family work.

Another economic idea, "resource-bargaining theory" focuses on power in families.[21] This theory suggests that understanding the division of childcare or housework in families requires understanding partners' bargaining power. Most individuals are self-interested and prefer to do less onerous or low-status tasks. Childcare is often viewed as low-status work, as exemplified by the low salaries paid to childcare workers in the United States. Parents who earn a higher income than their spouses are in a stronger position to bargain their way out of doing childcare or housework. Women tend to work in lower paid jobs and therefore have less economic bargaining power in the family. Researchers have found limited support for this theory. For example, studies have shown that men who earn about the same income as their spouses perform more housework than men who are primary breadwinners, but men who earn considerably less income than their spouses do not perform more housework than men who are primary breadwinners.[22]

Feminist researchers have also contributed to our under-standing about fathers' involvement with children. At the heart of feminist theory is the idea of "doing gender."[23] Doing gender refers to the ways in which individuals create gender in their everyday interactions with one another. For example, fathers and mothers cocreate gendered relationships through the actions they take to do housework and care work. The choices that fathers and mothers actively make to divide household and childcare tasks reproduce gendered relationships. They may choose to repro-duce traditional gendered relationships by assigning childcare to mothers and breadwinning to fathers, or they may choose a less traditional approach by dividing tasks equally. Feminists also suggest that the institutions in society play an important role in promoting behavior that is normally attributed to gender.[24] For example, mothers are almost always more involved in children's schools because those institutions expect mothers' participation and have low expectations for fathers' participation. According to feminist theory, fathers and mothers behave more similarly if they are exposed to similar expectations in society.[25] This theo-retical perspective is interesting because it suggests that fathers' and mothers' choices to divide childcare tasks are influenced by forces outside the family.

Feminist theory and social constructionist theory also sug-gest than men and women actively construct or make their own reality of what it means to be a father.[26] Each man and woman has a distinctive point of view about what it means to be a father. But the social construction of fatherhood does not take place in a vacuum. How men and women construct the meaning of fatherhood is influenced by experiences in their community and family of origin as well as by the broader society (e.g., exposure to social media). For example, fathers' ideas about masculinity play an important part in the social construction of fathering. Men who have traditional ideals about being a man will tend to believe that their main role is to provide financially for the family, with childcare is secondary. Men who have less traditional ideals about masculinity will tend to believe that they should be highly involved in caring for children.

## Developmental Theories

**Ecological-systems Theory.** Ecological-systems theory is used in this book to guide our discussion of children's development and the influence of fathers on children. The ecological-systems perspective tells us that children's development is determined by multiple factors, including those in the immediate environment of the child and those that are more distant.[27] There is no one factor that explains how children develop. Figure 1.1 illustrates how the ecological-systems perspective works. Children's immediate environment consists of parents, schools, siblings, and other family members. These influences are called microsystem influences. Children are not "blank slates" whose development is solely dependent on their immediate environment. Children influence their own development and they influence those around them. In essence, it is the interplay of children's own characteristics (e.g., genetic predispositions, child sex at birth) and their environment that determines how they develop and grow. For example, there is ample evidence that children's development is positively affected by fathers' involvement with them, but at the same time, the sex of the child influences how involved fathers become with the child. Studies have found that daughters receive more attention from fathers than sons.[28]

More distant environments, also known as macrosystems, influence children's development as well. We frequently do not think about how macrosystems influence parenting, but they can

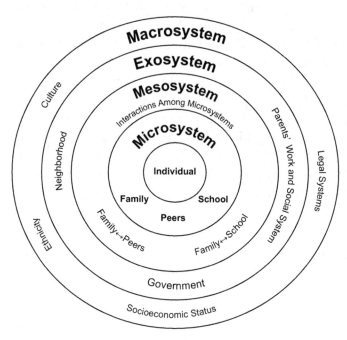

**FIGURE 1.1** Ecological-systems Theory

have a profound influence on children. For example, paternity leave is an important macrosystem variable that affects fathers' involvement with newborns. Paternity leave allows fathers to take leave from their jobs (paid or unpaid) to care for newborns. Fathers who have access to paternity leave and who take longer periods of leave are more engaged with their young children and are more committed parents.[29] Most countries offer some paternity leave, although the amount of time varies from two weeks of paid leave (e.g., Estonia) to one full year of partial pay in Japan. Paternity leave is limited to 12 weeks of unpaid leave in the United States, although some employers provide additional or paid leave. Many studies have shown support for the ecological-systems perspective, including influences at all levels of the environment.[30]

**Family Systems Theory.** According to family systems theory, families are groups of individuals organized into interdependent subsystems, including mother–father, mother–child, father–child, mother–father–child, and sibling subsystems.

Grandparents, aunts, and uncles may also be members of family systems if they are engaged in significant ways with the family. The subsystems exert direct and indirect influence on one another. For example, the mother–father subsystem influences the father–child subsystem and vice versa. Families do not need to consist of two parents and their biological children living in one household to function as a system. Family systems may exist as nuclear families, single parent families, blended families, extended families, and so forth.

Parents are the family's executive subsystem because they are the key organizers of the family environment. The mother–father subsystem comprises interactions between two adults that are focused on the spouse/partner relationship (i.e., marital quality) as well as interactions that are focused on parenting and children, also known as coparenting.[31] The spouse/partner and coparenting relationships overlap with one another. A major difference between spouse/partner relationships and coparenting is that partner relationships involve exchanges that are not focused on children, whereas coparenting interactions involve exchanges that are always focused on children.[32] Coparenting interactions often occur in the context of interacting with the child and are conducted with the child's well-being in mind. In contrast, partner interactions that are unrelated to the parenting role often take place outside the view of children and focus greater attention on the couple relationship.

The quality of fathers' relationships with their spouses or partners influences fathers' involvement with children. Loving and happy relationships between partners provide a supportive context in which parents can feel more successful in the parenting role and better handle the day-to-day stresses of parenting.[33] Fathers who are satisfied with their marital relationship have been found to be more positively engaged with children.[34] Similarly, positive coparenting relationships between fathers and mothers are strong predictors of father involvement.[35] Fathers are more involved with children when they and their partners support each other's parenting, work together as a team, work out disagreements about childcare and parenting, and engage in relatively low levels of conflict over children.

## Diverse Contexts of Fatherhood

People often think of fathers as a single homogeneous group of individuals. That is very much not the case. We have already indicated that culture, race, and ethnicity can influence fathers. Fathers and their relationships with children also vary based on whether the man lives with his child, the status of the man's relationship with the child's mother (divorced, married, cohabiting), and whether the man is a biological, adoptive, or stepfather. Children may have two fathers who are gay and married or unmarried. Children may also have a transgendered father whose sex at birth was female but who now identifies as a man. There are also stay-at-home fathers, foster care fathers, and godfathers. This book could not possibly do justice to a discussion about each of these subgroups of fathers. We focus, instead, on one subgroup of men—those who do not live with their biological children—because they are one of the largest subgroups of fathers. The term used to describe these men is *nonresident fathers.*

About 26% of children in the United States did not reside with their biological fathers in 2019.[36] These statistics included children who did not live with biological fathers because their parents were separated, divorced, or never married. Nonresident fathers, like all fathers, are a diverse group. There are some children who do not live with their fathers because the man is incarcerated, in the military, or working a long distance from where the child resides. Although many nonresident biological fathers are involved with their children and see them on a regular basis, a substantial number of fathers have no contact with their children. According to the most recent data. from 2007, 17% of nonresident fathers did not visit their children in the past year.[37]

We emphasize throughout this book that context matters. Parenting when you do not live with children can be challenging. Fathering after a divorce is different from fathering when one is never married. Legally, men are presumed to be the father when they are married at the time of the child's birth. That is not the case with unmarried fathers. Unmarried fathers who do not establish legal paternity do not have the right to visit the child, obtain custody, or make decisions for the child. (We discuss establishing paternity in greater detail in Chapter 2.)

The father's relationship with his child's mother is one of the most significant contextual factors contributing to divorced and unmarried nonresident fathers' involvement with children. Rebecca Ryan and colleagues found that nonresident fathers who were in continuously romantic relationships with mothers were significantly more likely to be involved with children than nonresident fathers who were not romantically involved with the mother.[38] Nonresident fathers are also more likely to be involved with children when they have positive coparenting relationships with the mother,[39] consistently pay child support to the mother if there is a support order,[40] and do not have children with multiple partners.[41]

It is important to note that nonresidence does not equate with fathers' noninvolvement with children. One of the authors of this book (Jay) conducted a study to determine whether low-income nonresident fathers' contact with children during early childhood was associated with the same children's reports of closeness to fathers at age 9 years.[42] About one third of children who never lived with their fathers at ages 1, 3, 5, and 9 had regular contact with the father, one third had no contact, and one third had intermittent contact with the father. Nine-year-old children reported closer relationships to their nonresident fathers when they had regular contact with the father during the early years despite not living together. They also had closer relationships with fathers when they started to see the father at age 5 after never seeing them at ages 1 and 3. The lesson learned from this research is that nonresident fathers should make every effort to become involved with their children right after birth. It is never too late to become involved and establish a relationship with one's child, but involvement with one's child during early childhood leads to a closer father–child relationship. As we will show in Chapter 2, becoming involved before the child's birth (during the pregnancy) is important, too. Nonresident fathers should do everything possible to work out their differences with mothers even if they are no longer in a romantic relationship, reach out to others for support and guidance, and engage in self-reflection so that they can become an involved father from the very start. Many fathers manage to have positive coparenting relationships despite no longer being romantic partners, and when coparenting relationships are positive, fathers have many more opportunities to be involved with children.

How does the saying go: "Once a father, always a father." This saying may sound cliché, but it is nonetheless worthy of consideration, both for fathers who do not live with their children and fathers who do live with their children. Parenting does not end when children turn 18 years old. Fathers are parents for as long as they live. As we will show in this book, there are many ways in which fathers influence their children. It is undoubtedly one of the most important roles, and perhaps the most important role, that a man can assume in his life. Men's own growth and development is impacted by the time and effort that they put into fathering. We hope this book will help fathers as they make their way along the amazing journey of parenthood.

## Notes

1 Pittman, F. S. (1994). *Man enough: Fathers, sons, and the search for masculinity.* Perigee.
2 Fagan, J., Day, R., Lamb, M., & Cabrera, N. (2014). Should researchers conceptualize fathering and mothering differently? *Journal of Family Theory and Review, 6,*390–405. https://doi.org/10.1111/jftr.12044
3 Randles, J. (2018). "Manning up" to be a good father: Hybrid fatherhood, masculinity, and U.S. responsible fatherhood policy. *Gender & Society, 32*(4), 516–539. https://doi.org/10.1177/0891243218770364
4 Randles, J. (2018). "Manning up" to be a good father.
5 Goodwill, J. R., Anyiwo, N., Williams, E. D. G., Johnson, N. C., Mattis, J. S., & Watkins, D. C.
6 Slade, A., Sadler, L. S., Eaves, T., & Webb, D. L. (2023). *Enhancing attachment and reflective parenting in clinical practice.* Guildford Press.
7 Pleck, J. H. (2010). Paternal involvement: Revised conceptualization and theoretical linkages with child outcomes. In M. E. Lamb (Ed.), *The role of the father in child development* (5th ed., pp. 58–93). Wiley.
8 Lamb, M. E., Pleck, J. H., & Levine, J. A. (1987). A biosocial perspective on paternal behavior and involvement. In C. Lewis & M. O'Brien (Eds.), *Reassessing fatherhood: New observations on fathers and the modern family* (pp. 109–125). Sage.
9 Pleck, J. H. (2010). Paternal involvement.
10 Morman, M. T., & Floyd, K. (2002). A "changing culture of fatherhood": Effects on affectionate communication, closeness, and satisfaction in men's

relationships with their fathers and sons. *Western Journal of Communication*, 66(4), 395–411. https://doi.org/10.1080/10570310209374746

11 Hofferth, S. L., & Phillips, D. A. (1987). Child care in the United States, 1970 to 1995. *Journal of Marriage and the Family*, 49(3), 559–571. https://doi.org/10.2307/352201

12 LaRossa, R. (1997). *The modernization of fatherhood: A social and political history*. University of Chicago Press.

13 The American Time Use Survey (ATUS) study consists of noninstitutionalized individuals ages 15 and older residing in occupied households in the United States. Fathers who do not reside with their children are not included in the study sample. U.S. Bureau of Labor Statistics. (2022). *American Time Use Survey Summary*. www.bls.gov/news.release/atus.nr0.htm; Converse, P. E., & Robinson, J. P. (1980). *Americans' use of time: 1965–1966*. Interuniversity Consortium for Political and Social Research.

14 Hayes, S. (1996). *The cultural contradictions of motherhood*. Yale University Press, p. 8.

15 Cha, Y., & Park, H. (2021). Converging educational differences in parents' time use in developmental child care. *Journal of Marriage and Family*, 83, 769–785. https://doi.org/10.1111/jomf.12720

16 Tichenor, V., McQuillan, J., Greil, A. L., & Shreffler, K. M. (2011). The importance of fatherhood to U.S. married and cohabiting men. *Fathering: A Journal of Theory Research and Practice about Men as Fathers*, 9(3), 232–251. https://doi.org/10.3149/fth.0903.232

17 Kuo, P. X., Volling, B. L., & Gonzalez, R. (2018). Gender role beliefs, work–family conflict, and father involvement after the birth of a second child. *Psychology of Men & Masculinities*, 19, 243–256. http://dx.doi.org/10.1037/men0000101

18 Levine, J., & Pittinsky, T. L. (1997). *Working fathers: New strategies for balancing work and family*. Addison-Wesley.

19 Nielsen, L. (2018). Joint versus sole physical custody: Children's outcomes independent of parent–child relationships, income, and conflict in 60 studies. *Journal of Divorce & Remarriage*, 59, 247–281. https://doi.org/10.1080/10502556.2018.1454204

20 Sayer, L. C. (2016). Trends in women's and men's time use, 1965–2012: Back to the future? In S. M. McHale et al. (Eds.), *Gender and couple relationships* (pp. 43–77). SpringerLink. https://doi.org/10.1007/978-3-319-21635-5_2

21 Blood, R. O., Jr., & Wolfe, D. M. (1960). *Husbands and wives: The dynamics of family living*. Free Press of Glencoe.

22 Thébaud, S. (2010). Masculinity, bargaining, and breadwinning: Understanding men's housework in the cultural context of paid work. *Gender & Society*, 24(3), 330–354. https://doi.org/10.1177/0891243210369105

23 Doucet, A., & Lee, R. (2014). Fathering, feminism(s), gender, and sexualities: Connections, tensions, and new pathways. *Journal of Family Theory and Review*, 6, 355–373. https://doi.org/10.1111/jftr.12051

24 Risman, B. J. (1989). Can men "mother"? Life as a single father. In B. J. Risman & P. Schwartz (Eds.), *Gender in intimate relationships* (pp. 155–164). Wadsworth Publishing.

25 Risman, B. J., & Schwartz, P. (1989). Being gendered: A microstructural view of intimate relationships. In B. J. Risman & P. Schwartz (Eds.), *Gender in intimate relationships* (pp. 1–9). Wadsworth Publishing.

26 Dienhart, A. (1998). *Reshaping fatherhood: The social construction of shared parenting* (Understanding Families series, 1st ed.). Sage.

27 Bronfenbrenner, U., & Morris, P. A. (2006). The bioecological model of human development. In W. Damon & R. M. Lerner (Eds.), *Handbook of child psychology, Vol. 1: Theoretical models of human development* (6th ed., pp. 793–828). Wiley.

28 Harris, K. M., & Morgan, S. P. (1991). Fathers, sons, and daughters: Differential paternal involvement in parenting. *Journal of Marriage and Family, 53*(3), 531–544. https://doi.org/10.2307/352730

29 Petts, R. J., & Knoester, C. (2018). Paternity leavetaking and father engagement. *Journal of Marriage and Family, 80,* 1144–1162. https://doi.org/10.1111/jomf.12494

30 Hofferth, S. L. (2003). Race/ethnic differences in father involvement in two-parent families: Culture, context, or economy? *Journal of Family Issues, 24*(2), 185–216. https://doi.org/10.1177/0192513X02250087; Icard, L. D., Fagan, J., Lee, Y., & Rutledge, S. E. (2017). Father's involvement in the lives of children in foster care. *Child & Family Social Work, 22,* 57–66. https://doi.org/10.1111/cfs.12196; Kulik, L., & Sadeh, I. (2015). Explaining fathers' involvement in childcare: An ecological approach. *Community, Work & Family, 18*(1), 19–40. https://doi.org/10.1080/13668803.2014.944483

31 Brown, G. L., Schoppe-Sullivan, S. J., Mangelsdorf, S. C., & Neff, C. (2010). Observed and reported coparenting as predictors of infant–mother and infant–father attachment security. *Early Child Development and Care, 180,* 121–137. https://doi.org/10.1080/03004430903415015

32 Palkovitz, R., Fagan, J., & Hull, J. (2013). Coparental considerations in understanding, researching and facilitating father involvement and children's wellbeing. In N. Cabrera & C. Tamis-LaMonda (Eds.), *Handbook of father involvement* (2nd ed., pp. 202–219). Lawrence Erlbaum Associates.

33 Bradford, K., & Hawkins, A. J. (2006). Learning competent fathering: A longitudinal analysis of marital intimacy and fathering. *Fathering: A Journal of Theory, Research, and Practice about Men as Fathers, 4,* 215–234. http://dx.doi.org/10.3149/fth.0403.215

34 Skinner, O. D., Sun, X., & McHale, S. M. (2021). Links between marital and parent–child relationship in African American families: A dyadic approach. *Journal of Family Psychology, 35*(8), 1086–1096. https://doi.org/10.1037/fam0000844

35 Palkovitz, R. et al. (2013). Coparental considerations.

36 Anderson, L. R., Hemez, P. F., & Kreider, R. M. (2022). Living arrangements of children: 2019. United States Census Bureau. www.census.gov/content/dam/Census/library/publications/2022/demo/p70-174.pdf

37 Livingston, G., & Parker, K. (2011). A tale of two fathers: More are active but more are absent. Pew Research Center. www.pewresearch.org/social-trends/2011/06/15/a-tale-of-two-fathers/

38 Ryan, R. M., Kalil, A., & Ziol-Guest, K. M. (2008). Longitudinal patterns of nonresident fathers' involvement: The role of resources and relations. *Journal of Marriage and Family, 70,* 962–977. https://doi.org/10.1111/j.1741-3737.2008.00539.x

39 Fagan, J., & Palkovitz, R. (2011). Coparenting and relationship quality effects on father engagement: Variations by residence, romance. *Journal of Marriage and Family, 73,* 637–653. https://doi.org/10.1111/j.1741-3737.2011.00834.x

40 Hofferth, S. L., Forry, N. D., & Peters, H. E. (2010). Child support, father–child contact, and preteens' involvement with nonresidential fathers: Racial/ethnic differences. *Journal of Family and Economic Issues, 31*(1), 14–32. https://doi.org/10.1007/s10834-009-9172-9

41 Fagan, J., Pearson, J., & Kaufman, R. (2019). A descriptive study of low-income never married fathers' coparenting with mothers and relatives. *Family Relations: An Interdisciplinary Journal of Applied Family Studies, 69,* 21–35. https://doi.org/10.1111/fare.12384
42 Fagan, J. (in press). Children's contact with fathers who never co-resided with them and father-child relationship quality at age 9. *Journal of Family Issues.* https://doi.org/10.1177/0192513X23122003

# 2

# Fathers and Pregnancy

## Great Expectations

*My first feeling is excitement. I am definitely looking forward to raising a child and carrying on what my parents did for me. How things work, taking me to pee wee soccer, learning to read, color, all of those things. I am definitely looking forward to reliving those moments through my own child. ... I know the effects of a having a newborn are going to be taxing, and I am a little anxious about how that might affect my relationship with my wife. Any time there is more stress in the situation, it is more difficult, but the excitement ... is definitely outweighing any anxiety that I am feeling now.*

*The OBs have definitely been helpful. In person, they will address any questions I have. I have tried to attend as many of the appointments that I can. ... It has been a really great experience. As a father, there has definitely been [the sense that] you are not the patient. The way the health care system is set up, it helps my wife when she calls the hotline to ask specific questions, and on occasion, I have gotten some hesitation from the nurses about providing that information directly to me. ... As a father, you are not treated as ... the patient. [The nurses] can offer resources for people you can talk to, but it is clear you are not the patient. I think that at times if you have a question about the pregnancy or concerns you might have ..., those are not the people you can go and ask. You probably have to go outside of the OBGYN process. ... You have to go and seek that help as a father. It is not provided as part of the overall health care package. If an OBGYN practice had a counselor for fathers to talk to, that would be a huge positive.*

—Interview with a father of an unborn child

## Introduction

Many men think that real fathering begins after their child is born. That is very much not the case—fathering begins well before the child's birth. Expecting a new baby has long been thought of as the sole domain of mothers, but that is not true. As

DOI: 10.4324/9781003486107-2

the quote from the father interview at the beginning of the chapter shows, men have many thoughts and feelings about becoming a father and their experience with pregnancy.

Father's roles in prenatal development are influenced by many factors, including the relationship between the mother and father and whether the pregnancy was intended. In the United States in 2018, 45% of pregnancies were unintended.[1]

When fathers learn of their partner's pregnancy, their responses will vary depending upon the circumstances. Some fathers will be ecstatic, as they have been waiting for this next stage of their family life. Others are relieved that a pregnancy has finally happened. When a pregnancy has not been planned, fathers may be surprised, happy, ambivalent, upset, anxious, or fearful about how this may change their life.[2] No matter what the intentions were, there are some common developmental tasks that fathers need to consider as they approach how to best support their partner and unborn child during pregnancy.

The roles fathers play are crucial during this time because of the vulnerability of the unborn child and the transition to a new coparenting relationship with the child's mother that begins during pregnancy. The growing body of research about how to protect unborn children informs us that fathers can be proactive and a positive influence on the pregnancy and birth.[3] Fathers' potential as protectors during pregnancy has been established by recent research on the impact of father's attitudes and behaviors on both mothers and unborn children.[4]

Some psychologists write about men's readiness for fatherhood. Getting married or cohabiting with a partner is viewed by many men as a step toward fatherhood. Selection of an intimate partner may be partially based on a man's perception that his partner is interested in having children. All men bring the experience of their own father's presence or absence as a foundational template for thinking about fatherhood. Some men talk about their lack of a good role model for fatherhood. There may be men other than a biological or adoptive father who have been role models in men's lives, often referred to as "social fathers." Some men had a stepfather or mother's new partner who lived with and cared for them as social fathers. Other men who served as role models may include an uncle, grandfather, or someone outside the family such as a teacher, coach, or minister. The lack of a positive role model can be a barrier to men who may know what *not* to do but don't understand what good fathers actually *do*. It is important for men to prepare for fatherhood by engaging in self-reflection about becoming a father.

## Reflection Questions

- ◆ Who are my role models for being a good father? What have I learned from them?
- ◆ What are the strengths that I bring to this new role?
- ◆ What kind of father does my child need?

In addition to self-reflection, men can prepare for fatherhood by spending time caring for or taking responsibility for children. This may involve spending time with a niece or nephew, coaching sports with children or youth, working as a camp counselor, or caring for a child in the neighborhood as a babysitter. Experiences in caring for and teaching children may inspire men to want to become a parent. However, boys and men in our society often are not prepared for parenthood in the same way that girls and women are. Most men also have limited exposure to classes or books about parenting prior to parenthood. One of the authors (Glen) taught a Parent–Child Relations class that met a requirement for general education at the college level. In a typical class of 40 students there were only 1 or 2 men. When teaching parenting classes to fathers over the course of 40 years, whenever Glen asked how many men had taken a child development or parenting class or read a book on parenting, only a small percentage reported having these experiences. Men often discount knowledge and experiences that prepare for parenthood because they think parenting is learned best through hands-on experience. While most men have a positive attitude and look forward to becoming a parent, their socialization for this role is limited by competing interests and activities. Pregnancy is an essential time for men to prepare for the new responsibilities of parenthood.

This chapter focuses on the important roles that expectant fathers can play to directly support the mother's health and well-being, the well-being of the unborn baby, and prepare for the birth. The father also becomes part of a new family system and creates his own identity as a father. The new roles that fathers incorporate into their identity include being a parenting partner, nurturer, provider, protector, and role model. Another section of the chapter addresses challenges some fathers may face and support systems to help them to cope with these challenges.

## Building a Parenting Partnership

Expectant fathers can start their preparation for fatherhood by establishing a coparenting relationship with the child's mother. Coparenting has been defined as parents working together to meet the child's needs.[5] The coparenting relationship starts during pregnancy and evolves throughout the child's life.[6] Coparenting includes expectant fathers and mothers talking and making decisions about the child's name, deciding whether or not the mother will breastfeed, establishing a budget for how much will be spent on baby furniture and clothing, deciding how involved in-laws and other relatives will be in caregiving, and much more. This is a time when fathers and mothers begin to talk about sharing parenting responsibilities. Fathers and mothers often have conversations with each other about work commitments and work and family balance. Finding and selecting childcare can also be part of these discussions.

Laurie A. van Egeren has written that coparenting has both internal and external dimensions.[7] The internal dimension is represented by each parent's feelings that their partner validates their parenting judgments and is committed to the child's well-being. The external dimension is manifested through parents' actual coparenting interactions with each other. These interactions can be harmonious, hostile, or competitive as they discuss how they plan to parent together. They can also be characterized by differences in how parents are invested in the child. Mothers are frequently more invested, while fathers may be less certain about their new roles and responsibilities.

During the pregnancy, fathers become aware of mothers' expectations for their involvement with the child. Fathers' and mothers' expectations for father involvement may differ. Fathers may feel their role is to be the primary breadwinner in the family. Mothers may feel that their own career is being sacrificed and expect more involvement and support from fathers so they can work. These differences can lead to conflict and hostile feelings. Parents may be reluctant to talk about their expectations, but it is important to do so during pregnancy to minimize conflicts and disappointments when the baby arrives. This is a time for clear communication and negotiation of how to share new roles and responsibilities related to raising a child. Building a parenting alliance during this time will help to alleviate stress during pregnancy and create a positive image of coparenting that works for both parents.

One of the authors of this book (Jay) has conducted a study to examine the extent to which fathers and mothers agree about their roles and their coparenting relationship before the child's birth.[8] Jay interviewed young fathers and mothers to find out if they had different perceptions of their parenting alliance during pregnancy. They often did not agree about the quality of their alliance. He found that fathers tended to perceive the quality of the parenting alliance more positively than mothers did. Jay explained that young fathers may be overly idealistic before the birth about the extent to which they will be able to work together with the mother as a team. Their experiences with forming a parenting alliance may change dramatically once the baby arrives and the father experiences the responsibilities of caring for a newborn. Studies such as this one indicate that fathers and mothers need to talk to each other about their coparenting relationship during the pregnancy. A good starting point is to ask one's partner, "Do you think the two of us are on the same page about how to care for our baby?" and "How are we going to share parenting responsibilities for the physical care of our baby?"

## Preparation for Fatherhood

Most fathers want to learn about pregnancy, prenatal development, and childbirth.[9] They have questions about when the sex of the child becomes known, what mothers should or should not eat or drink to keep the unborn baby safe, mothers' discomfort and pain during pregnancy, hormonal changes in women, labor and delivery, possible complications, and their role during childbirth. Interviews with expectant fathers have suggested that men often do not know what is expected of them during pregnancy.[10] Not knowing what to expect leaves many fathers feeling anxious and uncertain. Anne Howarth and colleagues found that knowledge about pregnancy and childbirth helps fathers to feel supported and calm and improves satisfaction.[11] However, men often feel excluded in their contacts with professionals because childbirth and parent education tend to focus on women and motherhood and do not address fathers' concerns.[12] In reality, prenatal health care services are for mother and the unborn baby and that is how services are designed and billed. Fathers are the "missing link" in prenatal care.[13] In a childbirth preparation class that Glen attended with his wife in 1977, a few fathers had a side conversation during a break in the class. They wondered, "Will the class talk about fathers and our anxieties and emotions?" None of them wanted to appear self-centered or weak and did not press the issue with the female instructor. It was not part of the class— no time was given to the topic. We hope that this has changed, but our fear is that the fast pace of life for working parents does not allow time and space for these discussions.

It is often assumed that fathers should support mothers during pregnancy and not receive support themselves. Studies with expectant fathers have shown that men need support as well.[14] Philip Boyce and his colleagues interviewed 312 first-time expectant Australian fathers about their stress during the pregnancy.[15] Stress, anxiety, and depression were not uncommon among the men. Some expectant fathers increased their alcohol consumption during the pregnancy. Boyce and colleagues suggested that men's fears and anxieties during pregnancy may be related to expectations that they will need to relinquish a carefree, independent lifestyle and adopt the responsibilities and restrictions of the parent role. Men benefit from support to manage their own anxieties and understand the challenges and rewards of creating a new identity as a family man and involved father.

Chris May and Richard Fletcher articulated the specific content that fathers are interested in learning to help address their needs[16]: They want to learn about the development of the unborn baby. This helps men understand the amazing process of prenatal development and how their own behaviors may influence this process. Fathers also want and need to understand the mother's thoughts and feelings and how they can be most supportive. May and Fletcher suggested that fathers should also develop an awareness of the risk for developing postpartum depression in both mothers and fathers and how to seek help if this occurs. Pregnancy is also a time to understand the importance of male nurturance and the development of caregiving skills. Fathers can benefit from learning about infant crying patterns and specific techniques to soothe babies to help prevent them from becoming overwhelmed by a crying baby. This list describes information a father should know to help negotiate the typical concerns of expectant fathers.

Parent education classes designed specifically for fathers have become more prevalent during recent years, but they are still uncommon. Expectations for father involvement keep expanding, but the resources to guide men through learning how to meet these expectations are limited. Boot Camp for New Dads is the largest program for new fathers in the United States, and is now offered in 44 states and on U.S. military bases, as well as in Canada and the United Kingdom (https://www .bootcampfornewdads.org/). This program is a father-to-father, community-based, one-time workshop that aims to increase fathers' knowledge and confidence during pregnancy and as a new parent and helps them support their partners and successfully transition to parenthood. There is no specific curriculum in Boot Camp for New Dads; instead, expectant fathers meet with other fathers who have just had a baby and are encouraged to ask questions. The program focuses specifically on fathers and promotes discussion and mutual support among fathers.

Programs such as Boot Camp for New Dads can help expectant fathers to obtain knowledge about pregnancy, childbirth, and caring for a new baby. There are also a few programs that have emerged that target coparenting and the transition to parenthood. Family Foundations (famfound.net) is a universal parenting education and coparenting program that meets for eight weeks from the third trimester through the first months after birth.[17] The program content is also available on DVD to make it more accessible to parents. There are also responsible fatherhood programs that provide support to help men manage their new roles and responsibilities as they aspire to be involved fathers—check fatherhood.gov for more information.

Researchers have found that many fathers seek information about pregnancy and childbirth on the internet. There are many resources available to expectant parents about these topics, but there is also much misinformation on the internet. Fathers are advised to ask their health care providers to suggest the best websites for expectant parents to get the most up-to-date information and advice.

## Fathers' Participation in Prenatal Care

Tova Walsh has interviewed fathers and mothers about fathers' participation in prenatal care.[18] She found that fathers are interested in participating in prenatal care sessions and also attend sessions because their partners ask them to come. The fathers in her study liked hearing about the mother's pregnancy and development of the fetus directly from care staff rather than learning second hand from mothers. Fathers also said that hearing their baby's heartbeat at a routine prenatal appointment or seeing the baby on the screen at an ultrasound examination was a powerful emotional experience for them. When asked about what they would change during the visits, fathers wished that providers would be more direct and specific with important information, because they do not always know what questions to ask.

Many fathers attend appointments that include an ultrasound. Fathers and mothers tend to view the screening as a social event rather than a medical screening.[19] The sonogram provides the first opportunity to see the baby. This can be a "magic moment" for fathers, when the idea of a baby becomes a concrete reality. Parents view the event with joy and anticipation. Parents are often presented with a copy of the ultrasound that they can show to relatives and friends. Expectant fathers said that the ultrasound image makes the baby more real to them.[20]

Researcher Jan Draper found that fathers rarely consider that the ultrasound may provide bad news.[21] Mothers and fathers expect to hear that their baby is normal. Parents' expectations can be shattered by bad news during an ultrasound.[22] Shock and grief can occur, intensified by expectations for having a healthy baby. Mothers and fathers said that they wanted the sonographer to be open and honest with them and they were upset when they felt that knowledge about their baby was being withheld.[23]

## Supporting the Mother

Supporting mothers is a critical role for fathers during pregnancy. Fathers provide support to mothers in many ways. They join the mother during prenatal visits and help prepare the home for the arrival of the baby. Men often like building things, and mothers feel supported when fathers help prepare the baby's bedroom. Fathers can do additional housework when the mother is tired or feeling overwhelmed. Margareta Widarsson and colleagues reported that mothers feel supported when fathers express understanding and try to be a calming influence.[24] Childbirth education classes can be very helpful to fathers as they learn to be the mother's labor and delivery partner and as a formal support system to help mother and father prepare for the birth experience. Supporting one's partner during the pregnancy signals that the father feels a strong emotional connection to the mother as a coparent.

Fathers' support of mothers during labor and delivery is essential. Hospital labor and delivery rooms opened to fathers in the mid-1970s. Studies show that 93% of resident fathers across ethnic groups were present at the time of birth in the United States.[25] Fathers can support their partners by attending to their physical needs in the delivery room, such as helping them change positions, communicate with medical staff, or keep warm or cool, as well as giving massages, cuddling, and providing fluids if the mother asks.[26] Fathers can also serve as emotional support, helping to regulate the mother's emotions. The National Charity for Pregnancy, Birth and Early Parenthood in the United Kingdom suggests that fathers and mothers should prepare a birth plan[27] by talking about mothers' preferences during labor and delivery. Mothers are less able to discuss their preferences as labor progresses and mothers and fathers are both overwhelmed with the pain and emotions of childbirth. The components of a birth plan are outlined in Text Box 2.1 as a guide to discussion of parents' preferences. Each birth is unique, however, and the birth plan is not a set of rigid rules to follow if unexpected events happen and the plan doesn't fit.

---

**TEXT BOX 2.1**

Birth plans should include:

◆ The place of birth
◆ Who will be with the mother-to-be
◆ What role the birth partner would like to play
◆ Mobility during labor
◆ Coping strategies, such as changing positions, massage, and breathing that you may have practiced as a couple in childbirth education classes
◆ Pain relief
◆ What to do if intervention is required
◆ Who will hold the baby first
◆ Who will cut the cord
◆ Breastfeeding and skin-to-skin contact

Source: NCT (National Charity for Pregnancy, Birth and Early Parenthood) (n.d.).

## Reflection Questions

◆ What can I do to support my partner's physical health during pregnancy?

◆ What can I do to minimize the stress that my partner is experiencing?

◆ What can my partner and I do together to prepare for the new baby?

## Bonding with the Unborn Baby

Preparing for fatherhood is not just about developing a coparenting relationship with the mother, obtaining knowledge, participating in prenatal appointments, and providing support to mother. It also involves development of a relationship with the unborn baby.[28] Pregnancy activates fathers' emotional bond with the child, developed through the father's capacity to form a relationship with an "imagined" baby.[29] Ellen Galinsky refers to pregnancy as the image-making stage of parenthood.[30] Visualizing oneself as a father—perhaps feeding, holding, and diapering the baby—is a part of this relationship development. Fathers may think about what the baby will look like after he or she is born.

Early relationship bonds also develop when fathers interact with the unborn baby in the mother's belly. Fathers may feel the baby move in the mother's abdomen. They may talk or sing to the baby (e.g., telling him or her about yourself). Looking at the baby's ultrasound can also engender strong feelings of attachment to the baby. Some fathers create pet names for their unborn child that reflect their growing attachment and their image of their child's personality. Researchers have found that fathers who are more emotionally engaged in these types of bonding behaviors interacted more positively with the child at age 4 months than fathers who were emotionally disengaged during the pregnancy.[31]

Fathers may fear they won't be able to become emotionally attached or care for the baby. It is common for expectant fathers to have dreams where they worry about hurting the new baby. Glen had a dream that he was carrying his new baby and dropped him in the street. When he picked up the baby, he had turned into the Disney character Goofy—a sure sign of serious injury. A few dream steps later, he stumbled and dropped Goofy, who was now totally deflated. No deep dream interpretation is needed here; anxiety about being a capable caregiver to a fragile new baby is obvious. Imagining fathering the baby and developing a relationship with the unborn baby can help ease fathers' anxieties.

## Fathers' Prenatal Involvement Strengthens Engagement with Children

Men who are involved in the pregnancy are more likely to be engaged with their newborns and infants.[32] Jay has studied this issue with low-income fathers. He found that low-income unmarried fathers who supported the mother during the pregnancy and attended prenatal visits were significantly more likely to be engaged with their 1- and 3-year-old children.[33] Jay and his colleagues suggested that fathers who become involved during the pregnancy are more committed to becoming a parent, they bond with the unborn child, and they make positive life changes, including committing themselves to a relationship with the child's mother and accepting the responsibility to be gainfully and stably employed.

Jay wanted to know if fathers' prenatal involvement had long-lasting effects on fathers' involvement with children. He and his colleagues found that unmarried fathers' prenatal support of the mother and presence at the birth were directly related to their engagement with 5-year-old children and higher levels of child-reported closeness to the father at ages 9 and 15 years.[34] The authors concluded that early prenatal support and engagement puts men on a trajectory of positive parenting that extends well into the child's teenage years.

## Expectant Fathers' Contributions to a Healthy Birth

There is increasing recognition than men contribute to a healthy birth experience in numerous ways. According to Milton Kotelchuck and Michael Lu, even men's health before the baby is conceived is crucial for improving pregnancy outcomes because it enhances men's biologic and genetic contributions to pregnancy.[35] A baby's health can be negatively affected when men have preconception diabetes, elevated lead levels in their blood, or smoke tobacco.[36] The Centers for Disease Control report that men's smoking can also result in fertility problems by damaging sperm and contributing to impotence.[37]

There is ample evidence that mothers' smoking during pregnancy can have negative effects on the baby. Fathers' smoking during pregnancy also contributes to poor health in the baby. Research conducted in India found that babies born to mothers exposed to second-hand smoke during pregnancy had significantly lower mean birth weight, lower mean length at birth, and lower mean birth head circumference compared to babies whose mothers were not exposed to second-hand smoke.[38] When both parents smoke, there is greater risk for shorter mean length at birth than when only mothers or fathers smoke.[39] Fathers can be a positive support for mothers by choosing not to smoke as a way to protect their unborn child.

There are many practical ways that fathers can support healthy lifestyles that benefit both the mother and the unborn child. They can help mothers choose to eat healthy foods and get sufficient sleep.[40] They can avoid preparing foods that exacerbate morning sickness. They can help by lifting heavy objects and doing housework during the pregnancy. These activities demonstrate support and help to lessen stress in mothers, which directly impacts the health of the unborn child.[41]

## Building a New Identity as a Father

Pregnancy is a time when many fathers, especially first-time fathers, engage in self-reflection. They reflect on what kind of parent they want to become and their roles as providers, caregivers, husbands/partners, sons, and friends. This self-reflection can include making a commitment to become an involved father, deciding to prioritize work and become a good provider, deciding to prioritize one's relationship to the expectant mother, and downplaying one's relationship with friends in favor of being an involved father and coparent. Men's self-reflection does not take place in isolation; it may take place in conjunction with conversations with wives/partners or other fathers. Employers can have an impact when they encourage men to work harder or climb the career ladder as new fathers. Friends who have children may look forward to the man's entry into parenthood so they can share experiences as parents. Men's reevaluation can also take place in the context of changing societal expectations. The older paternalistic role of fathers only as moral guides has given way to the expectation that involved fathers will be nurturers and caregivers, as well as role models, for their children.

Men's transition to parenthood is one of the most demanding periods of psychological reorganization of the self.[42] At this time, men build a new identity or sense of self, defined by values and beliefs, ethnicity, gender, and social roles. They may decide that being a father now takes precedence over work or that being a husband/partner is more important than spending a lot of time with friends. This identity may change over time, especially when the new baby arrives.

The integration of the social roles of father, provider, husband/partner, son, and friend into a new identity is a challenging developmental task. The media and popular literature give the impression that men are either highly involved primary caregiving fathers or completely absent fathers,[43] but this is a false dichotomy. There is great variation in the extent to which fathers choose to be involved with their children. While a small group of stay-at-home dads has emerged, the traditional role of provider still dominates as the primary responsibility for most fathers.

Building a new identity may be more challenging for men who have not followed the more traditional paths of developing a work identity or career and finding a partner before having a child. A recent review of studies found that the formation of a new identity is stressful for most fathers because they worry about being a "good father" and "getting it right."[44] We want to emphasize here that there is no single way to be a father. Some men prioritize fatherhood over work while other men prioritize work over fatherhood. These variations in identity may be influenced by many factors, including the man's upbringing, age, and relationship with his wife/partner.

## Challenges Faced by Unmarried and Nonresidential Fathers

In Chapter 1 we wrote that context plays an important role in fathers' involvement with children. Most expectant fathers experience joy and excitement during the transition to parenthood. But some men do not feel ready to have children or they may have mixed emotions about having a child or about their relationship with the child's mother. Kathy Edin and her colleagues found that these emotions are especially true of low-income fathers who were unmarried at the time of their child's birth: eight out of ten low-income, unmarried fathers experienced mixed emotions about the pregnancy.[45]

In the United States, about 40% of children are born to unmarried mothers. Many unmarried fathers coreside with their child and the child's mother. For the most part, these fathers are just as involved with children as married fathers are, despite many having uncertain or negative feelings about the pregnancy. Some unmarried fathers do not coreside with their children. Nonresidence can be a barrier to fathers who would like to have a relationship with their child but begin with no legal rights and have to depend upon keeping a good relationship with the mother to have access to and spend time with their child. These fathers are often faced with barriers in addition to not having legal status as a father. They often struggle with unemployment and underemployment, their relationships with partners are less stable, they have fewer social supports than other men, and a disproportionate number of this group of fathers have criminal justice histories. The Ludwig Institute for Shared Economic Prosperity estimated the True Rate of Unemployment (TRU) for low-income men in January 2020 was 23.5%, which was seven times higher than the official unemployment rate of 3.6% defined by the U.S. Bureau of Labor Statistics.[46] Although researchers have debated how unemployment influences men's transition to parenthood, it is clear that unemployment and underemployment place low-income, unmarried men on a path of having child support obligations that they often cannot meet as they try to support themselves in a separate household from their children. Not all low-income, unmarried fathers have child support obligations. Mothers can choose not to petition the court for child support, but if they apply for public assistance (TANF) they have no choice but to file for child support.

A court order establishing paternity is necessary if an unmarried mother is applying for child support. Establishing paternity is easiest when it is done in the hospital at birth. Both parents voluntarily sign a form establishing the father's paternity when the birth is registered. As long as the form is signed at this time, no DNA testing is required and there is no need for a court order. One advantage of in-hospital paternity establishment is that the biological father's name is included on the birth certificate. There are additional benefits associated with paternity establishment—children are eligible for benefits through their fathers, including health insurance, life insurance, Social Security, veteran's benefits, and inheritance. In instances where the child is referred to child welfare because of abuse or neglect, fathers who have established paternity have the right to receive notice of court proceedings regarding the child, petitions for adoption, and actions to terminate parental rights.[47] It is helpful for fathers in these more complex situations to be aware of the laws and find advocates to help them with paternity and establishing parenting time.

## Reflections for Expectant Fathers

Fathers often do not identify the values they hope will guide them as they become role models for their child.[48] What is important to teach your child? What are the values that you and your partner want to pass on to your child? This may also be a time to think about your relationship with your own father. How do you want to be the same or different from him or from your mother? If you have moved away from earlier religious beliefs and practices, being an expectant father may trigger a renewed interest in thinking about religious and moral values.

## Reflection Questions

◆ What kind of relationship do I hope to create with my child?

◆ What values guide me as I seek to be an involved father?

◆ Where can I talk about my feelings, worries, and concerns as an expectant father?

## Summary

Fathers play an important role in the health and well-being of their unborn child. The support provided to the mother helps to ensure the health and well-being of the child. Fathers also need support during the pregnancy, as they have many questions about pregnancy, childbirth, and caring for newborns. Fathers often report that the health care system does not do enough to provide the support that they need. Pregnancy is a time when many fathers engage in self-reflection and reevaluation of their identity. Community supports and programs can help men to manage their new roles and responsibilities.

## Notes

1 Guttmacher Institute. (2019). Unintended pregnancy in the United States. https://www.guttmacher.org/fact-sheet/unintended-pregnancy-united -states

2 Hanson, S., Hunter, L. P., Bormann, J. R., & Sobo, E. J. (2009). Paternal fears of childbirth: A literature review. *The Journal of Perinatal Education, 18*(4), 12–20. https://doi.org/10.1624/105812409X474672

3 Inoue, S., Naruse, H., Yorifuji, T., Kato, T., Murakoshi, T., Doi, H., & Subramanian, S. V. (2017). Impact of maternal and paternal smoking on birth outcomes. *Journal of Public Health, 39*(3), 1–10. https://doi.org/10.1093 /pubmed/fdw050; Kotelchuck, M., & Lu, M. (2017). Father's role in precon- ception health. *Maternal and Child Health Journal, 21,* 2025–2039. https://doi .org/10.1007/s10995-017-2370-4

4 Giurgescu, C., & Templin, T. N. (2015). Father involvement and psychological well-being of pregnant women. *MCN American Journal of Maternal and Child Nursing, 40*(6), 381–387. https://doi.org/10.1097/NMC.0000000000000183

5 Van Egeren, L. A., & Hawkins, D. P. (2004). Coming to terms with coparenting: Implications of definition and measurement. *Journal of Adult Development, 11,* 165–178. https://doi.org/10.1023/B:JADE.0000035625.74672.0b

6 Van Egeren, L. A. (2004). The development of the coparenting relationship over the transition to parenthood. *Infant Mental Health Journal, 25,* 453–477. https://doi.org/10.1002/imhj.20019

7 Van Egeren, L. A. (2004). The development of the coparenting relationship over the transition to parenthood.

8 Fagan, J. (2014). Adolescent parents' partner conflict and parenting alliance, fathers' prenatal involvement, and fathers' engagement with infants. *Journal of Family Issues, 35*(11), 1415–1439. https://doi.org/10.1177/0192513X13491411

9 Howarth, A. M., Scott, K. M., & Swain, N. R. (2019). First-time fathers' perception of their childbirth experiences. *Journal of Health Psychology, 24*(7), 929–940. https://doi.org/10.1177/1359105316687628

10 Widarsson, M., Engström, G., Tydén, T., Lundberg, P., & Hammar, L. M. (2015). "Paddling upstream": Fathers' involvement during pregnancy as described by expectant fathers and mothers. *Journal of Clinical Nursing, 24,* 1059–1068. https://doi.org/10.1111/jocn.12784

11 Howarth, A. M., Scott, K. M., & Swain, N. R. (2019). First-time fathers' perception of their childbirth experiences.

12 Plantin, L., Olykoya, A., & Ny, P. (2011). Positive health outcomes of fathers' involvement in pregnancy and childbirth paternal support: A scope study literature review. *Fathering: A Journal of Theory, Research, and Practice about Men as Fathers, 9*(1), 87–102. https://doi.org/10.3149/fth.0901.87

13 Bond, M. J. (2010). The missing link in MCH: Paternal involvement in pregnancy outcomes. *American Journal of Men's Health, 4*(4), 285–286. https://doi.org/10.1177/155798831084842

14 Poh, H. L., Koh, S. S. L., & He, H.-G. (2014). A review of fathers' experiences. *International Nursing Review, 61,* 543–554. https://doi.org/10.1111/inr.12137

15 Boyce, P., Condon, J., Barton, J., & Corkindale, C. (2007). First-time fathers' study: Psychological distress in expectant fathers during pregnancy. *Australian & New Zealand Journal of Psychiatry, 41*(9), 718–725.

16 May, C., & Fletcher, R. (2013). Preparing fathers for the transition to parenthood: Recommendations for the content of antenatal education. *Midwifery, 29,* 474–478.

17 Feinberg, M. E., & Kan, M. L. (2015). Family foundations. In M. J. Van Ryzin, K. L. Kumfer, G. M. Fosco, & M. T. Greenberg (Eds.), *Family-based prevention programs for children and adolescents* (pp. 35–53). Psychology Press.

18 Walsh, T. B., Carpenter, E., Costanzo, M. A., Howard, L., & Reynders, R. (2021). Present as a partner and a parent: Mothers' and fathers' perspectives on father participation in prenatal care. *Infant Mental Health Journal, 42,* 386–399. https://doi.org/10.1002/imhj.21920

19 Draper, J. (2002). "It was a real good show": The ultrasound scan, fathers and the power of visual knowledge. *Sociology of Health & Illness, 24,* 771–795. https://doi.org/10.1111/1467-9566.00318

20 Åhman, A., Lindgren, P., & Sarkadi, A. (2012). Facts first, then reaction— Expectant fathers' experiences of an ultrasound screening identifying soft markers. *Midwifery, 28*(5), e667–e675. https://doi.org/10.1016/j.midw.2011.07.008

21 Draper, J. (2002). "It was a real good show."

22 Denney-Koelsch, E. M., Côté-Arsenault, D., & Lemcke-Berno, E. (2015). Parents' experiences with ultrasound during pregnancy with a lethal fetal diagnosis. *Global Qualitative Nursing Research, 2,* 2333393615587888. https://doi.org/10.1177/2333393615587888

23 Denney-Koelsch, E. M., et al. (2015). Parents' experiences with ultrasound.

24  Widarsson, M., et al. (2015). "Paddling upstream."
25  Bronte-Tinkew, J., Ryan, S., Carrano, J., & Moore, K. A. (2007). Resident fathers' pregnancy intentions, prenatal behaviors, and links to involvement with infants. *Journal of Marriage and Family, 69*(4), 977–990. https://doi.org /10.1111/j.1741-3737.2007.00425.x
26  Kainz, G., Eliasson, M., & von Post, I. (2010). The child's father, an important person for the mother's well-being during the childbirth: A hermeneutic study. *Health Care for Women International, 31*(7), 621–635. https://doi.org/10 .1080/07399331003725499
27  NCT [National Charity for Pregnancy, Birth and Early Parenthood]. (n.d.). www.nct.org.uk/about-us/vision-mission-and-goal
28  Doan, H., & Zimmerman, A. (2003). Conceptualizing prenatal attachment: Toward a multidimensional view. *Journal of Prenatal and Perinatal Psychology & Health, 18*, 131–148.
29  Lindstedt, J., Korja, R., Vilja, S., & Ahlqvist-Björkroth, S. (2021). Fathers' pre-natal attachment representations and the quality of father–child interac-tion in infancy and toddlerhood. *Journal of Family Psychology, 35*(4), 478–488. https://doi.org/10.1037/fam0000813
30  Galinsky, E. (1987). *The six stages of parenthood.* Addison-Wesley.
31  Lindstedt, J., et al. (2021). Fathers' prenatal attachment.
32  Cabrera, N. J., Shannon, J. D., West, J., & Brooks-Gunn, J. (2006). Parental interactions with Latino infants: Variation by country of origin and English proficiency. *Child Development, 77*(5), 1190–1207. https://doi.org/10.1111/j .1467-8624.2006.00928.x
33  Cabrera, N., Fagan, J., & Farrie, D. (2008). Explaining the long reach of fathers' prenatal involvement on later paternal engagement with children. *Journal of Marriage and Family, 70*, 1094–1107.
34  Fagan, J., Cabrera, N., & Ghosh, R. (2022). Explaining the long reach of prena-tal behaviors and attitudes in unmarried men at birth on father engagement in early and middle childhood and adolescence. *Developmental Psychology.* Advanced online publication. https://doi.org/10.1037/dev0001471
35  Kotelchuck, M., & Lu, M. (2017). Father's role in preconception health.
36  García Esquinas, E., Aragonés, N., Fernández, M. A., García Sagredo, J. M., de León, A., de Paz, C., Pérez-Meixeira, A. M., Gil, E., Iriso, A., Cisneros, M., de Santos, A., Sanz, J. C., García, J. F., Asensio, Á., Vioque, J., López-Abente, G., Astray, J., Pollán, M., Martínez, M., … Pérez-Gómez, B. (2014). Newborns and low to moderate prenatal environmental lead exposure: Might fathers be the key? https://doi.org/10.1007/s11356-014-2738-6; Moss, J. L., & Harris, K. M. (2015). Impact of maternal and paternal preconception health on birth outcomes using prospective couples' data in Add Health. *Archives of Gynecology and Obstetrics, 291*(2), 287–298. https://doi.org/10.1007 /s00404-014-3521-0
37  Centers for Disease Control. (2014). *Smoking and reproduction.* www.cdc.gov /tobacco/sgr/50th-anniversary/pdfs/fs_smoking_reproduction_508.pdf
38  Prince, P. M., Umman, M., Fathima, F. N., & Johnson, A. R. (2021). Secondhand smoke exposure during pregnancy and its effect on birth outcomes: Evidence from a retrospective cohort study in a tertiary care hospital in Bengaluru. *Indian Journal of Community Medicine, 46*(1), 102–106. https://doi.org/10.4103/ijcm.IJCM_464_20
39  Inoue, S., et al. (2017). Impact of maternal and paternal smoking on birth outcomes.

40 Garzon, I. (2022). Dad's role during the pregnancy. www.bellybelly.com.au/pregnancy/dads-role-during-the-pregnancy/

41 Kinsella, M. T., & Monk, C. (2009). Impact of maternal stress, depression and anxiety on fetal neurobehavioral development. *Clinical Obstetrics Gynecology, 52*(3), 425–440. https://doi.org/10.1097/GRF.0b013e3181b52df1

42 Genesoni, L., & Tallandini, M. A. (2009). Men's psychological transition to fatherhood: An analysis of the literature. *Birth, 36*(4), 305–318. https://doi.org/10.111/j1523-536X2009.00358x

43 Habib, C., & Lancaster, S. (2006). The transition to fatherhood: Identity and bonding in early pregnancy. *Fathering: A Journal of Theory, Research, and Practice about Men as Fathers, 4*(3), 235–253. https://doi.org/10.3149/fth.0403.235

44 Baldwin, S., Malone, M., Sandall, J., & Bick, D. (2018). Mental health and wellbeing during the transition to fatherhood: A systematic review of first time fathers' experiences. *JBI Database of Systemic Reviews and Implementation Reports, 16*(11), 2118–2191. https://doi.org/10.11124/JBISRIR-2017-003773

45 Edin, K., England, P., & Linnenberg, K. (2003, September). *Love and distrust among unmarried parents.* Presentation at the National Poverty Center Conference, Washington, DC.

46 Ludwig Institute for Shared Economic Prosperity. (2020). *Measuring better: Development of "True Rate of Unemployment" data as the basis for social and economic policy.* https://assets.websitefiles.com/5f67c16a6ca3251ecc11eca7/5fd77b946b8ccc555b8cc6e5_November%20White%20Paper%201220.pdf

47 Child Welfare Information Gateway. (2017). *The rights of unmarried fathers.* www.childwelfare.gov/pubpdfs/putative.pdf

48 Palkovitz, R., & Palm, G. (1998). Fatherhood and faith in formation: The developmental effects of fathering on religiosity and values. *The Journal of Men's Studies, 7*(1), 33–51.

# 3

# Transition to Fathering

## Welcoming Baby

*I was a very social person before my daughter was born. Now, it is all about her. We don't have time to do those things that we used to do in the past. It's like growing up. You miss parts of that, but at the same time, it doesn't compare to what I have gotten out of raising her so far. I would take it any day. ... We are a little more homebodies now. Her bedtime is 7:00, and she is very much on schedule. We are going out at 5:00 tonight. Usually that would be an 8:00 thing. Those are the biggest differences.*

*As a person you become almost immediately more responsible. Just to use an example, money. You have to be more responsible when it comes to spending. I never really made a budget in my life. Now you have to make a budget. Maturing in general. You can think you are ready for it, but it is such a change. The day that she was born, you are never really ready for it. I've grown in that sense. ... You read all these books before the baby is born. You take what you can ... . But then every child is so different. ... I think we have done a really good job of adapting to her ... . We have feelings about when she has to go off formula, when she should start solids, what she should be eating ... . You can try to feed your child as healthy as you want. At the end of the day, they eat what they want. The way that you grow ... you have to grow with them.*

—*Father of a 15-month-old daughter*

## Introduction

Most fathers are present at the births of their children and start this new journey with a range of emotions—from joy, amazement, and excitement to fear and anxiety—depending upon the birth circumstances. These are emotional and memorable moments that start a new chapter in the life of being a father. In a parenting class, Glen once asked a group of fathers of young children

DOI: 10.4324/9781003486107-3

to share the birth story of their child. Each father shared a clear recollection of their child's birth; a couple of weeks were needed to finish everyone's stories. Over the years, Glen has asked hundreds of fathers the question, "What was it like to hold your baby for the first time?" This memory brings a smile to their faces and for many, "It was the best day of my life!" Thus begins the face-to-face introduction to a new baby for fathers as the images created during pregnancy become a reality.

Infancy is the stage of life between birth and the emergence of language, sometime between ages 12 and 18 months. Infants rely completely on parents to meet their survival, emotional, and social needs, and they have many needs—they must be fed, burped, held, played with, rocked, put to sleep, diapered, cuddled, taken to the doctor, and introduced to the world.

Soon after birth, the infant recognizes the mother's voice. The baby recognizes the mother's voice before the father's voice because the infant in the womb frequently hears the mother speak. By the end of the third month, the infant can discriminate between the parents' faces and those of strangers. By the end of the first year, the child has intense feelings towards specific people. Parents are faced with continual challenges to understand and respond to their baby's cries, vocalizations, facial expressions, and body language.[1]

The father who was quoted at the beginning of this chapter described how life changes dramatically when there is a new baby. The infant is likely to occupy the father's thoughts throughout the day. Fathers may think about how the baby is doing or how mother is managing with the baby when they are away at work. Fathers may miss the baby and wish they were back home. Some fathers' preoccupation with baby may distract them at work, while other fathers may look forward to going to work and back to a world they know. Fathers must adjust to the baby's feeding and sleep schedules, as interrupted sleep can contribute to sleep deprivation and daytime sleepiness. Fathers who take paternity leave may have thoughts about work and worry about job security or the effect of taking leave on their career. Fathers experience changes in relationships with partners and other family members, lifestyle, and sense of self. Fathers also face new opportunities for learning and personal growth and development. They learn to care for the new baby and develop a trusting relationship. Fathers build a coparenting relationship, exploring new ways of sharing responsibility for baby care and supporting the mother–child relationship. Most fathers continue to work and explore ways to balance work with new family responsibilities. Finally, fathers have the opportunity to integrate new parenting and family roles into their identity as men.

This chapter addresses: (a) changes in men as they become fathers, (b) understanding typical tasks for fathers of newborns, and (c) understanding fathers' unique influences on development and implications for parenting practices.

## Changes in Fathers

The focus of most research on fathers has been on their importance and their influence on child development.[2] A less-explored area is the changes in men as they become new fathers.[3]

### Hormonal and Brain Changes

Recent research has begun to look at the behavioral, hormonal, and brain changes in men as they become fathers.[4] Fathers appear to display changes to specific areas of their brains (such as the network that facilitates empathy) related to their becoming new fathers and spending time with their babies.[5] Changes in hormones in new fathers, while not as dramatic as those in mothers, are related to changes in brain activity and in parenting behaviors. The hormone vasopressin appears to influence protective behaviors in fathers. New fathers who spend time with their infants experience a decrease in testosterone, which is connected to a decrease in aggression. Research indicates that the hormone oxytocin increases in fathers after childbirth and is correlated to less hostility and higher quality play between father and baby.[6] The research on changes in hormonal levels and brain size and structure reflect the influence of new fathers and babies on each other. Our understanding of specific parenting behaviors and where and how they are connected in the brain is still evolving.

## Values Changes

Another area of change in new fathers is related to their values. Glen worked with colleague Rob Palkovitz to conduct a qualitative study that focused on how fatherhood influenced adult development.[7] Rob, a developmental psychologist, was interested in exploring how becoming a father influenced men's thinking and behaviors. One of the questions in the study focused on shifts in values since becoming a father. Close to 80% reported changes in basic values—the most common being, "I am less selfish and more concerned about my child's needs." This line of research is related to the identity changes described in Chapter 1 on expectant fathers—becoming a father can be a time of examining values, a time of profound change. Glen has asked the question about shifts in values in his parenting groups during the last 30 years and continues to hear the same basic themes: Fathers report being less self-centered, more responsible, moving away from risky behavior, and thinking more about their actions as role models. This change in values is also reflected in fathers' attitudes about parenting taking priority over work.[8] Most men understand and aspire to these expectations, but fathers may struggle to meet them due to work commitments, lack of role models, and ideas in society that do not value fathering. Nonetheless, changes in cultural expectations for fathers have resulted in greater father involvement and emotional availability. The early years of parenthood create an opportunity for men to explore their values, discover new pathways to empathy with their babies and toddlers, and consider their new responsibility to be a role model.

One way to support fathers' exploration of basic values and their relationships with their very young children is to help them reflect on their thoughts and feelings about fatherhood. Here are several questions for fathers to reflect on as they consider changes in themselves and remember their own parents' practices and what they may want to keep or change.

## Reflection Questions

- ◆ How has fatherhood changed your view of your parents?
- ◆ What are some ways you want to be similar to or different from your father? From your mother?

- ◆ How has fatherhood created shifts in your values or what is most important in life?
- ◆ How has fatherhood changed how you feel about yourself as a person?

## Developmental Tasks for Fathers

The next section of this chapter focuses on developmental tasks of new fathers. The first part considers the initial experience of bringing your infant home from the hospital and learning about care for newborns. The second part reviews the attachment process and how fathers become confident attachment partners. The third part focuses on establishing a coparenting alliance.

### Caring for Newborns and Infants

The first task that fathers face after taking their babies home is to learn how to care for a newborn. There are many decisions that parents face in determining how to care for their baby. An early decision is how to feed the baby. One of the most important things fathers can do is to support mothers' breastfeeding. Breastfeeding is healthier for infants than formula. Breastmilk is biologically designed for human babies to provide optimal nutrition and support their immune system and gut.[9] Children receive many benefits from breastfeeding: they are less likely to become obese; they are more physically fit,[10] and they have better cognitive outcomes.[11] Breastfeeding also benefits mothers, who experience reduced risk of breast and ovarian cancer, osteoporosis, heart disease, and diabetes compared to mothers who do not breastfeed.[12]

The influence that fathers have on mothers' breastfeeding is a good example of the ecological systems perspective, which we introduced in Chapter 1. This perspective emphasizes that children are influenced by the many contexts in which they live. Fathers' support of breastfeeding indirectly influences and benefits babies through the support they give to mothers.

Despite the benefits, studies of first-time fathers found that men often did not know how to support their partner when she experienced breastfeeding difficulties.[13] Breastfeeding was also associated with increased anxiety in fathers. They often reported that health professionals did not provide adequate levels of information and support to them.[14] There are many ways in which fathers can support mothers' breastfeeding. They can do housework, change diapers, bathe infants, and provide emotional support to mothers. Mothers also feel supported when fathers make efforts to learn about breastfeeding.[15] One study found that mothers were more likely to breastfeed for longer durations when fathers were supportive.[16] Fathers' supportiveness included responding sensitively and positively to mothers' breastfeeding, being patient and understanding of the time it takes to breastfeed, helping with breastfeeding-related activities, and showing pleasure and satisfaction while mothers breastfed the infant. Fathers may also encourage mothers to get help from other mothers or healthcare providers when breastfeeding becomes a challenge.

The U.S. Department of Agriculture WIC Program offers helpful ways in which fathers can support mothers' breastfeeding (see Text Box 3.1).[17]

---

**TEXT BOX 3.1**

**Supporting Mothers' Breastfeeding**

♦ Help take care of your baby
♦ Watch for baby's hunger signs
♦ Limit visitors
♦ Help with chores
♦ Offer encouragement
♦ Defend the choice to breastfeed
      Source: U.S. Department of Agriculture WIC Program (n.d.).

---

Many mothers go back to work while still breastfeeding. They may pump at work, which gives babies the continued benefits of breast milk. Pumping at home or at work can be challenging for mothers and may require additional support from fathers, especially if the mother's employer is indifferent or hostile to her desire to continue breastfeeding.

While fathers can support mothers in breastfeeding, not all mothers are able to breastfeed babies and sometimes babies need supplemental feedings. This allows fathers to be involved in bottle feeding the baby. Fathers can learn comfortable positions for bottle feeding by adjusting to their baby's cues around relaxed body position, quality of sucking, and when the baby is finished. The father's role is to support mother in what works best for mother, child, and the family. Fathers living in the United States would benefit from a national policy that ensures paid parental leave for both mothers and fathers to spend time with newborns and establish initial feeding and sleeping routines.

A second caregiving task for fathers is to learn ways to soothe a crying or fussy baby. Fathers may have to sort out the reasons why the baby is crying and then experiment with ways to soothe him or her. It takes time to recognize a baby's unique cues for hunger, tiredness, discomfort from a wet or soiled diaper, or physical distress (such as gas or an ear infection). A baby may be comforted by a parent's rocking, singing, pacing the floor, or taking a stroller or car ride. Other times, babies just need to cry, and parents need to be with them to help regulate their discomfort or emotional distress. It is most important for fathers to remain calm while trying to soothe a crying baby.

About one in four babies experience colic, defined as baby's crying that lasts for more than three hours per day, happens more than three days per week, and occurs for more than three weeks.[18] Colicky babies do not sleep well and they are very fussy. Colic does not mean that there is anything wrong with the baby or with the parents, and it usually stops when the baby is 3 to 4 months of age. Both fathers and mothers experience anxiety and distress when they have a baby with colic. Fathers' distress over a colicky baby is intensified when mothers experience higher levels of distress.[19] Parents need extra support from each other, pediatricians, family, and friends when they have a colicky baby.

Fathers and mothers often worry about caring for the baby. They worry about the baby's sleep, nutrition, and weight gain; and what to do when the baby is sick. They are frequently asked by others whether the baby is sleeping through the night. Helen

Ball suggests that this leads to misconceptions that babies should sleep through the night and that prolonged sleep should be achieved early, neither of which is the case.[20] Breastfed babies wake more during the night than babies who are not breastfed. Some fathers and mothers worry that their baby will die while sleeping from sudden infant death syndrome (SIDS). SIDS is very rare, occurring about 1 in every 2,000 live births in the United States.[21] Current research suggests that the risk of SIDS is greatly reduced when parents place their child on their backs while they sleep (remember "back to sleep"). Babies that experience sleep issues are challenging for parents, who also are not getting enough sleep. Fathers can help by sharing in developing sleep routines for baby and parents and by finding their own ways to comfort crying infants.

Other tasks for fathers include playing with the infant, encouraging vocalizations, changing diapers, giving baths, getting up at night for feedings (a father can change the baby and give her or him to the mother to breastfeed or feed baby a bottle), dressing them, and taking them on errands or outings. Researchers have found that first-time fathers engage in these caregiving tasks almost as much as mothers.[22] Second-time fathers engage in these caregiving activities somewhat less frequently than first-time fathers. Fathers vary in their desire to become involved in infant care, but for the most part, they interact tenderly with infants and are responsive to infants' needs. Developmental psychologists Charles Lewis and Michael Lamb have written that fathers learn quickly about the uniqueness of their newborns, although they tend to be somewhat less perceptive of the babies' needs than mothers.[23] The transition to fatherhood is an important time for fathers to reflect on their experience as a new parent.

## Reflection Questions

- ♦ What has been the most rewarding part of being a new dad?
- ♦ When did you first start to feel connected to you baby?
- ♦ How does your baby get and keep your attention?
- ♦ How has fatherhood changed some of your daily routines—eating, sleeping, screen time?

## Establishing Attachment

One of the most important developmental tasks during infancy and toddlerhood is the formation of the parent–child attachment relationship. Attachment is the long-term process of forming an intense and enduring relationship with an infant to protect them and meet their needs.[24] The attachment relationship between parents and children grows gradually during infancy and toddlerhood. Infants cry to elicit a response from parents when they are hungry, tired, experience physical discomfort, or when they need to be comforted and soothed. Crying encourages parents to approach, pick up, soothe, stay near, and feed the baby or otherwise meet their needs. During the first 2 months after they are born, babies focus on their internal functions and seek biological equilibrium to keep warm, nourished, rested, and regulate their digestive system. They may also recognize parents through familiarity with their voice or smell. At around age 2 months, babies come to prefer their parents or other regular caregivers. Over time, babies learn to trust and expect that their parents can be counted on to respond quickly to their needs. At around age 7 months, babies have strong preferences to interact with parents who have become their attachment figures who are consistently responsive to their needs. Attachment figures provide a sense of security to the child when he or she is fearful, frustrated, or startled.[25] The sense of security provided by the attachment figure can last throughout the child's life.[26]

Almost all young children develop attachments to parents or other caregivers. Developmental psychologists indicate that the quality of the attachment relationship matters most. Children whose parents respond consistently to their needs in a warm and nonhostile manner are more likely to develop a secure attachment to their parent. Although these children can become very distressed when separated from the parent, they are quickly comforted by the parent when they are reunited. Children who cannot rely on parents to consistently respond to their needs or whose parents respond in a hostile manner may develop an insecure attachment to the parent. These children protest when separated from the parent but then respond ambivalently or angrily when reunited with the parent.

A simple model of the attachment process as children move from infants to toddlers has been developed by the Circle of Security parenting program.[27] Glen has used this program for the past ten years in his work with incarcerated fathers. The simple circle model of children moving out to explore from a secure base and coming back to a safe haven for comfort or help in calming strong emotions describes the basic dynamics of attachment. Fathers in his class report that this helps them to remember to pay attention to their children's cues and also to reflect on their own emotions as they interact with their children.

**Father–Mother Differences**. Attachment research traditionally focused on mothers, with fathers as secondary attachment figures. Researchers began to take a closer look at fathers in the 1970s and established that fathers were also primary attachment figures and were sensitive to infant cues.[28] One obvious difference between mothers and fathers related to attachment is that mothers carry the unborn child for 9 months during the pregnancy. Mothers form a unique relationship with the unborn child that is evident after birth. One should not underestimate the significance of this early relationship between mothers and children. Mothers tend to be more protective of newborns because of the physical connection throughout the months of pregnancy. They are often the first to reach for the crying baby and the first to hear the baby awaken during the night. Mother–newborn relationships also develop quickly when mothers breastfeed their infants, which enables them to form a unique, intimate bond with their newborn. These early experiences help us understand why fathers may be less perceptive or sensitive than mothers. They also explain why some fathers feel mothers are better able to calm the baby.[29] In addition, infants often prefer their mothers to comfort them when they are distressed.[30] Fathers get a later start in forming a relationship with their baby and take a different path towards building their attachment relationship.

**Sensitivity and Synchrony**. The attachment research with fathers has examined two different core concepts—sensitivity and synchrony.[31] Sensitivity and responsiveness to infant cues are central to secure attachment to both mothers and fathers. However, the link for fathers is not as strong and there have been various explanations for these differences. Alice Rossi suggested that fathers are less sensitive to cues than mothers because mothers are usually the primary caregiver.[32] Daniel Paquette and Marc Bigras have suggested that the measures of sensitivity are based on mother–infant interactions and that measuring fathers' more playful style would be a better way to assess fathers' sensitivity.[33] This research suggests two possible implications: first, fathers might benefit from trying to be more sensitive and responsive to their babies while caring for them. Second, researchers could study fathers' pathways to secure attachment by measuring their playful interactions with their infants and their encouragement of exploration.

Fathers like to engage in "rough and tumble" play with children during late infancy and toddlerhood. Rough and tumble play refers to behaviors that appear aggressive (e.g., chasing or wrestling) but are performed in a playful, nonaggressive manner.[34] This type of play is enjoyable to infants and toddlers but can also become overwhelming if the child is over-stimulated. Fathers provide security to the child when they stop the play and help the child to calm down and set clear limits.

Attachment researchers have suggested that it does not take physical care (such as feeding or putting to bed) to establish an attachment relationship with the father; rather, attachment relationships can develop through regular and tender play between the infant and father.[35] The term "activation relationship" describes the emotional bond between fathers and children that enables the child to feel safe to take both physical and social risks and explore their environment.[36] The activation relationship theory, by taking into account the roles played by fathers, can help us to understand infant development. But fathers should be aware that rough and tumble play is of higher quality when it is warm, moderately controlling, sensitive, physically engaging, and playful.[37] When fathers interact with sensitivity and warmth, they provide a secure base for exploration and encourage children to go out into the world and then come back to share with fathers. We caution, however, that fathers should not only play with their infants and toddlers, but should also give sensitive physical care to their young children.

In addition to the concept of sensitivity, the idea of synchrony focuses on the interaction styles of parents. The metaphor of Dancing with Babies[38] helps parents understand synchrony and the different "dances" that fathers and mothers may do with their babies. Fathers in general are more tactile, physical, and arousing in their play with infants, while mothers are more verbal, didactic, and object-oriented.[39] Fathers have a more playful, jazzy style and more jagged rhythm, which both fathers and babies enjoy. This pattern seems to persist even for fathers who are the primary caregivers.[40]

Children acquire a greater sense of mastery during play when fathers are supportive. They help children to master playing with toys or objects that may frustrate them because they are difficult to manipulate. Karin Grossman and Klaus Grossman labeled these attachment-related behaviors as "secure exploration."[41] Supportive fathers help children to explore their environment and make new discoveries about how the world works.

To summarize major insights into fathers and the attachment process:

1. Fathers start out at a different place than mothers in creating an attachment relationship with their babies. They can begin to form a connection during the prenatal months as they observe their partners and begin to visualize their baby, especially after viewing a sonogram image. They can also begin to connect through talking, singing, or reading to their babies in utero as described in Chapter 1. This can help build a connection that is different from mom's experience.
2. Sensitivity to infant cues around needs is important for both fathers and mothers. Mothers appear to have an easier time picking up these cues. Fathers learn this skill with practice.
3. Fathers' pathway to connecting with their young children may center around their active style of play, which is a way that fathers interact, connect, and influence their children's development.

The important point is that fathers and their babies and toddlers find many dways to connect and form secure attachment relationships.

## Establishing a Coparenting Alliance

The family system is critically important for understanding fathers' involvement with children. The quality of the father–mother coparenting relationship is an essential component of a well-functioning family system. The coparenting relationship begins during the prenatal period, as explored in Chapter 2, when parents begin to work together to think about how to share parenting responsibilities, and continues to evolve after the arrival of the baby. The relationship between mothers and fathers after the birth of their child is an important factor that influences father–infant relationships. One of the developmental fathering tasks during the first year is to establish a parenting alliance with mothers that involves coordination and support between adults for the care and raising of their children.[42] This includes building a solid sense of support between parents, avoiding a pattern of antagonism and disruptions of parenting efforts, clarifying how best to divide up childcare time between parents, and mutual engagement of both parents in organizing and managing the daily lives and decisions around parenting.

Building a coparenting alliance has been described as a bumpy road during the first 3 years.[43] Mothers and fathers negotiate the new roles that they want to play in an ongoing manner that may be unique to each family system. Both mother and father need to agree about sharing of childcare tasks and child-rearing decisions and how to divide these in ways that work best for all involved. Fathers and mothers may find also that their own attitudes about child-rearing practices differ; negotiating parenting practices can be stressful. It takes extra effort on the part of both fathers and mothers to work against the social and economic norms to give fathers the time and space to learn new skills and gain confidence in this new role.

The patterns for this parenting alliance are set early in the transition to parenthood.[44] There are many factors that minimize the engagement of fathers during this transition and push parents into stereotypical gender roles. Ralph LaRossa and Maureen LaRossa identified this pattern in the late 1970s; multiple factors continue to push mothers to spend more time with new babies and limit the amount of time fathers have to get comfortable with their new babies.[45] Breastfeeding necessitates mother to be close to the baby during the first 6 months. Often income differences between men and women make it less feasible for fathers to take time off from work. Work and social pressures on both mothers and fathers push mothers into the role of primary parent. These factors tend to set up mother as child-rearing expert and make her reluctant to ask father to participate in caregiving work.[46] Even though the patterns of sharing child-rearing and care may solidify early during the transition to parenthood, there is no one pathway for making this division work for mothers, fathers, and children. Increasing fathers' direct contact and interaction with their new baby is an important goal. Fathers also indirectly impact development by supporting mother and creating a stable family system through their financial and emotional support for the benefit of the child. Fathers may want to reflect on the following questions about their coparenting relationships with mothers.

### Reflection Questions

- ◆ How has parenthood changed your relationship with your spouse/child's mother?
- ◆ What impact has parenthood had on your feelings of emotional closeness with your partner?
- ◆ How has parenthood changed how you spend time as a couple?
- ◆ In what ways do you and your child's mother support each other's parenting?

### Nonresident Fathers

Fathers who live with their children are intimately involved with the ups and downs of raising their young children. Fathers who do not live with the mother and their children have special challenges. Some nonresident fathers are highly involved with children, but many are not. Fathers who are involved infrequently with their children do not get to watch the mother breastfeed the baby, do not get to change diapers ten times per day, and may not experience the child's first smile, laugh, and many other developmental milestones.

There are many reasons that fathers do not live with their children, but in most instances, their nonresidence has something to do with breakdown in the relationship with the mother or the absence of a meaningful relationship with the mother when the baby was conceived. Mothers have considerable influence on the involvement of these fathers with their children through various aspects of the coparenting relationship. Maternal gatekeeping is considered by some researchers as one of the important coparenting mechanisms through which mothers influence fathers' involvement.[47] According to Jay (author of this book), maternal gatekeeping is defined as mothers' preferences and decisions to handle child-related matters themselves rather than sharing childcare with fathers.[48] Fathers who are uninvolved due to gatekeeping frequently report emotional pain because they want to be more involved with children.[49]

Nonresident fathers who see their infants and toddlers on a regular basis report that parenting is rewarding and enjoyable. Still, these fathers need to make sure that their commitment is for the long term. Nonresident fathers who remarry or have new partners may want to start a new life that excludes the child with whom they do not live. But children need their biological fathers even if the father starts a new family. The void that children feel when they are not involved with their father can be vast and have negative consequences for their development. The authors of this book have worked closely with fathers who do not live with their children and who struggle to stay connected to them. Our message is, "Don't give up." Work with the mother to create a collaborative relationship with her so that you can see your child. Listen to the mother if she feels you are not interacting with your child in a positive way. If you have a new partner or wife, talk with them about how important your child is to you. We discuss nonpayment of child support as a barrier to father involvement in Chapter 6.

There are many support groups that can help fathers to deal with the pain of not seeing their children. Fathers may need to go to family court to obtain visitation or custody rights. The process of going to court can be painful and expensive, but in the end, it can mean getting to see your child on a regular basis.

Nonresident fathers who are struggling to stay connected to their children should try to address the barriers to involvement as soon as possible. It is never too late to become an involved father, but having no contact with a child during the early months and years can mean that the father and child will not be as close to each other as the father would like to be. Address any barriers early.

## Summary

Like most other life transitions, becoming a father for the first time or becoming the father of another child is a major life event that can be both exhilarating and stressful. For first-time fathers, this transition means making significant lifestyle changes. Fathers must shift their focus from self-gratification to that of protecting and nurturing an infant who can survive and thrive only with care from parents. This is a time for self-reflection about one's values and about one's relationship with a partner and coparent. Fathering a newborn can be both joyful and challenging. It is also a time to support the baby's mother, learn about parenting a young child, and adapt to a family that now includes three or more individuals. Fathers who are sensitive, responsive, and engaged with their infants become important attachment figures for the child. The bonds formed between young children and fathers can last a lifetime and help to ensure the healthy development of the child.

## Notes

1 Bornstein, M. H., & Arterberry, M. E. (2022). *Infancy: The basics*. Routledge.
2 Pruett, K. D. (2000). *Fatherneed: Why father care is as essential as mother care for your child*. Broadway.
3 Palkovitz, R. (2002). *Involved fathering and men's adult development: Provisional balances*. Lawrence Erlbaum Associates.
4 Bakermans-Kranenburg, M., & van IJzendoorn, M. (2023). Sensitive responsiveness in expectant and new fathers. *Current Opinion in Psychology, 50*, 101580. https://doi.org/10.1016/j.copsyc.2023.101580
5 Abraham, E., Hendler, T., Shapira-Lichter, I., Kanat-Maymon, Y., Zagoory-Sharon, O., & Feldman, R. (2014). Father's brain is sensitive to childcare experiences. *PNAS, 111*(27), 9792–9797. https://doi.org/10.1073/pnas.140256911;

Kim, P., Rigo, P., Mayes, L. C., Feldman, R., Leckman, J. F., & Swain, J. E. (2014). Neural plasticity in fathers of human infants. *Social Neuroscience, 9*,522–535.https://doi.org/10.1080/17470919.2014.933713; Martinez-Garcia, M., Paternina-Die, M., Cardemas, S., Vilarroya, O., Desco, M., Carmona, S., & Saxbe, D. (2023). First-time fathers show longitudinal gray matter cortical volume reductions: Evidence from two international samples. *Cerebral Cortex, 33*, 4156–4163. https://doi.org/ 10.1093/cercor/bhac333

6 Grumi, S., Saracino, A., Volling, B., & Provenzi, L. (2021). A systematic review of human paternal oxytocin: Insights into the methodology and what we know so far. *Developmental Psychobiology, 63.* https://doi.org/ 10.1002/dev.22116

7 Palkovitz, R., & Palm, G. (1998). Fatherhood and faith in formation: The developmental effects of fathering on religiosity, morals, and values. *The Journal of Men's Studies, 7*(1), 33–51. https://doi.org/10.3149/jms.0701.33

8 Minnesota Fathers and Families Network. (2007). *Do we count fathers in Minnesota: Searching for key indicators of the well-being of fathers and families.* Author. e000001274.pdf

9 Shenker, N. (2019). The mysteries of milk RSB. www.rsb.org.uk//biologist -features/158-biologist/features/1758-the-mysteries-of-milk

10 Tambalis, K. D., Mourtakos, S., Panagiotakos, D. B., & Sidossis, L. S. (2019). Exclusive breastfeeding is favorably associated with physical fitness in children. *Breastfeeding Medicine, 14*, 390–397. https://doi.org/10.1089/bfm .2019.0043

11 Strom, M., Mortensen, E. L., Kesmodel, U. S., Halldorsson, T., Olsen, J., & Olsen, S. J. (2019). Is breast feeding associated with offspring IQ at age 5? Findings from prospective cohort: Lifestyle during Pregnancy Study. *BMJ Open, 9*, e023134. https://doi.org/10.1136/bmjopen-2018-023134

12 Rollins, N., Bhandari, N., Hajeebhoy, N., Horton, S., Lutter, C., Martines, J., Piwoz, E., & Richter, L. (2016). Why invest, and what it will take to improve breastfeeding practices? *The Lancet, 387*, 491–504. https://doi.org/10.1016/ S0140-6736(15)01044-2

13 Baldwin, S., Malone, M., Sandall, J., & Bick, D. (2018). Mental health and well-being during the transition to fatherhood: A systematic review of first-time fathers' experiences. *JBI Database of Systematic Reviews and Implementation Reports, 16*, 2118–2191. https://doi.org/10.11124/JBISRIR-2017-003773

14 Baldwin, S., et al. (2018). Mental health and wellbeing.

15 Tohotoa, J., Maycock, B., Hauck, Y. L., Howat, P., Burns, S., & Binns, C. W. (2009). Dads make a difference: An exploratory study of paternal support for breastfeeding in Perth, Western Australia. *International Breastfeeding Journal, 29*(4), 15. https://doi.org/10.1186/1746-4358-4-15

16 Rempel, L. A., Rempel, J. K., & Moore, K. C. J. (2017). Relationships between types of father breastfeeding support and breastfeeding outcomes. *Maternal & Child Nutrition, 13*, e12337. https://doi.org/10.1111/mcn.12337

17 U. S. Department of Agriculture. (n.d.). *How dads can support their breastfeeding partner.* https://wicbreastfeeding.fns.usda.gov/how-dads-can-support -their-breastfeeding-partner

18 John Hopkins Medicine. (n.d.). *What is colic?* www.hopkinsmedicine.org/ health/conditions-and-diseases/colic

19 de Kruijff, I., Veldhuis, M. S., Tromp, E., Vlieger, A. M., Benninga, M., & Lambregtse-van den Berg, M. P. (2021). Distress in fathers of babies with infant colic. *Acta Paediatrics, 110*, 2455–2461. https://doi.org/10.1111/apa .15873

20 Ball, H. L. (2013). Supporting parents who are worried about their newborn's sleep. *BMJ, 346*, 2344. https://doi.org/10.1136/bmj.f2344

21 Moon, R. Y., Horne, R. S. C., & Hauck, F. R. (2007). Sudden infant death syndrome. *The Lancet, 370*(9598), 1578–1587. https://doi.org/10.1016/S0140-6736(07)61662-6

22 Rustia, J. G., & Abbott, D. (1993). Father involvement in infant care: Two longitudinal studies. *International Journal of Nursing Studies, 30*(6), 467–476. https://doi.org/10.1016/0020-7489(93)90018-P

23 Lewis, C., & Lamb, M. E. (2003). Fathers' influences on children's development: The evidence from two-parent families. *European Journal of Psychology of Education, 18*, 211–228. https://doi.org/10.1007/BF03173485

24 Bowlby, J. (1982). *Attachment and loss: Vol. 1. Attachment* (2nd ed.). Basic Books.

25 Grossmann, K., & Grossmann, K. E. (2020). Essentials when studying child–father attachment: A fundamental view on safe haven and secure base phenomena. *Attachment & Human Development, 22*(1), 9–14. https://doi.org/10.1080/14616734.2019.1589056

26 Sroufe, L. A. (2005). Attachment and development: A prospective, longitudinal study from birth to adulthood. *Attachment & Human Development, 7*(4), 349–367. https://doi.org/10.1080/14616730500365928

27 Circle of Security International. (n.d.). *Resources for parents.* www.circleofsecurityinternational.com/resources-for-parents/

28 Lamb, M. E. (1977). Father–infant and mother–infant interaction in the first year of life. *Child Development, 48*(1), 167–181. https://doi.org/10.2307/1128896

29 Deave, T., & Johnson, D. (2008). The transition to parenthood: What does it mean for fathers? *Journal of Advanced Nursing, 63*, 626–633. https://doi-org.libproxy.temple.edu/10.1111/j 1365-2648.2008.04748.x

30 Grossmann, K., & Grossmann, K. E. (2020). Essentials when studying child–father attachment.

31 Palm, G. (2014). Attachment theory and fathers: Moving from "being there" to "being with." *Journal of Family Theory & Review, 6*(4), 282–297.

32 Rossi, A. (1984). Gender and parenthood. *American Sociological Review, 49*, 1–19. https://doi.org/10.4324/9781351329040-11

33 Paquette, D., & Bigras, M. (2010). The risky situation: A procedure for assessing the father–child activation relationship. *Early Child Development and Care, 180*(1–2), 33–50. https://doi.org/10.1080/03004430903414687

34 Pellegrini, A. D. (2002). Rough-and-tumble play from childhood through adolescence: Development and possible functions. In P. K. Smith & C. H. Hart (Eds.), *Blackwell handbook of childhood social development* (pp. 437–453). Blackwell.

35 Ainsworth, M. D. S., Blehar, M. C., Waters, E., & Wall, S. (1978). *Patterns of attachment. A psychological study of the strange situation.* Lawrence Erlbaum Associates.

36 Feldman, J. S., & Shaw, D. S. (2021). The premise and promise of activation parenting for fathers: A review and integration of extant literature. *Clinical Child and Family Psychology Review, 24*, 414–449. https://doi.org/10.1007/s10567-021-00351-7; Paquette, D. (2004). Theorizing the father–child relationship: Mechanisms and developmental outcomes. *Human Development, 47*(4), 193–219. https://doi.org/10.1159/000078723

37 StGeorge, J. M., Campbell, L. E., Hadlow, T., & Freeman, E. (2021). Quality and quantity: A study of father–toddler rough-and-tumble play. *Journal of*

*Child and Family Studies, 30*, 1275–1289. https://doi.org/10.1007/s10826-021 -01927-1

38  Thoman, E., & Browder, S. (1987). *Born dancing*. Harper & Row.

39  Brazelton, T. B. (1979). Behavioral competence of the newborn infant. *Seminars in Perinatology, 3*(1), 35–44.

40  Field, T. (1978). Interaction behaviors of primary versus secondary care-taker fathers. *Developmental Psychology, 14*(2), 183.

41  Grossmann, K., & Grossmann, K. E. (2020). Essentials when studying child–father attachment.

42  McHale, J. P. (2007). *Charting the bumpy road of coparenthood: Understanding the challenges of family life*. Zero to Three.

43  McHale, J. P. (2007). *Charting the bumpy road of coparenthood*.

44  McHale, J. P. (2007). *Charting the bumpy road of coparenthood*.

45  LaRossa, R., & LaRossa, M. M. (1981). *Transition to parenthood: How infants change families*. Sage.

46  Bakermans-Kranenburg, M., & van IJzendoorn, M. (2023). Sensitive responsiveness.

47  Schoppe-Sullivan, S. J., Brown, G. L., Cannon, E. A., Mangelsdorf, S. C., & Sokolowski, M. S. (2008). Maternal gatekeeping, coparenting quality, and fathering behavior in families with infants. *Journal of Family Psychology, 22*(3), 389–398. https://doi.org/10.1037/0893-3200.22.3.389

48  Fagan, J., & Barnett, M. (2003). The relationship between maternal gate-keeping, paternal competence, mothers' attitudes about the father role, and father involvement. *Journal of Family Issues, 24*, 1020–1043.

49  Fischer, R. A., Johnson, M. D., Stertz, A. M., Sherlock, S. N., & Wiese, B. S. (2023). How perceived maternal gatekeeping affects fathers: An 8-week study. *Journal of Family Psychology, 37*(2), 232–242. https://doi.org/ 10.1037/ fam0001053

# Fathers of Infants and Toddlers

## Building Connections and Nurturing Development

*It's remarkable what's happening every day. It's incredible to watch. She's learning new words and really understanding them. She's just beginning to fully walk. I can't put it fully into words. It's just amazing to see that happen. … I just enjoy spending time with her. … She's been in day care since 6 months. Being around other children that are walking and other stuff. … She gets to see that stuff before other children who have a nanny. She's a smart little girl. I think that plays a part in how quickly she's developing. I have to say, just watching her do the everyday things … .*

*[Most challenging is] the day care thing. She's gotten really sick a few times … constant colds. We've talked with other parents, and they say, when she goes to kindergarten or pre-school, she'll be the one who doesn't get sick. That's fine, but going through it is really tough. The other thing we find really challenging is having time for just the two of us. … There are times when you wish you could be doing a little bit more.*

*—Father of a 15-month-old daughter*

## Introduction

This chapter focuses on fathers and their influence on development of infants and toddlers. Fathers need to support their child's growth and development and manage their relationship with the child. One task of parents during the first three years is to understand how children develop. While there are typical milestones for development, it is important to understand that children develop at different paces based on their genetic predispositions, experiences, and interests. It is also useful for fathers to understand

DOI: 10.4324/9781003486107-4

what motivates infants and toddlers so they can model empathy and avoid power struggles. An infant's job is to connect to adults to get their needs met and then to begin to explore and experience the environment. Toddlers continue to explore their environment and begin to assert their independence and initiative. They also learn to express a variety of emotions, especially anger when they are frustrated in their attempts to master new tasks. They need the father's help in regulating their emotions. This often involves staying with a child rather than giving a time out and expecting a young child to manage big feelings on their own.

One challenge in considering child development during the first three years is the rapid pace of change. The transition to becoming a toddler happens between ages 12 to 18 months when infants learn how to walk and talk. Fathers who have learned to tune into the nonverbal cues of infants and respond to their needs find that they must adapt to the child's new interests in exploring while creating limits for safe exploration. Toddlers are mobile creatures who do not know how to keep themselves safe—and so are at a relatively high risk for unintentional injuries. According to the National Safety Council, the leading cause of death among 2-year-olds is drowning, followed by motor vehicle accidents.[1] Fathers play an important role in preventing unintentional injuries. Children ages 6 to 36 months are less likely to be injured when fathers are engaged in childcare tasks such as changing diapers and talking and reading to the child.[2] Fathers can prevent unintentional injuries by childproofing their home, which also reduces the need for constant parental supervision. The National Center for Fathering suggests that fathers should "crawl around your house and try to see the world as your child does".[3]

## Child Temperament

Parents typically become aware of a child's temperament during the first few months after birth. Temperament is a child's behavioral style—each child responds differently to their environment. Some are very active and express strong emotions, while others are passive, quiet, and easy to calm. For example, think about a child's crying. Some children cry very intensely and for long periods of time and are hard to soothe. Other children cry less intensely and are easy to soothe. How the baby tends to cry reflects the child's unique behavioral style. Ask any new parent if their child is easy or hard to manage and care for. Almost every parent can answer this question. The father who was quoted at the beginning of this chapter said that his child is extremely easy to manage. She rarely cries, and when she does, she is easy to soothe.

Children's temperaments are for the most part due to genetic predispositions and not the result of "bad" or "good" parenting. Together with parenting, culture, and environment, these predispositions play a major role in the development of the child's personality. Fathers and mothers who are not knowledgeable about temperament may think that their parenting causes their child's temperament but that is not the case.

The best way to understand temperament is to know the specific temperament characteristics of children. Text Box 4.1 describes temperament characteristics and their definitions.[4]

---

**TEXT BOX 4.1**

**Children's Temperament Characteristics**

- ◆ Activity level—energy level of the child
- ◆ Approach–withdraw—how the child responds to new settings and people
- ◆ Mood—the child's general tendency to be happy or unhappy
- ◆ Rhythmicity—how regular are the child's physical/biological patterns (e.g., eating, sleeping)
- ◆ Persistence—the child's ability to stay with a difficult task
- ◆ Attention span—the child's ability to focus on one task for a length of time
- ◆ Adaptability—the child's ability to adjust to changes in routine
- ◆ Threshold—the child's ability to handle external stimuli (e.g., loud noises)
- ◆ Intensity—the child's tendency to react strongly or less strongly to events
- ◆ Distractibility—the degree to which a child is easily distracted from a task or activity

    Source: Chess and Thomas (2016), *Temperament (theory and practice)*, Routledge.

Different temperament characteristics tend to cluster together in children. Some children's temperaments cluster into a group called *flexible*. These children have a high threshold, or tolerance, for environmental stimuli (e.g., loud noises), are low in intensity, have positive moods, adapt easily to new situations, and have regular rhythms. In contrast, some children are more *fearful*. They are slow to adapt to changes in the environment (such as being dropped off at childcare) and tend to withdraw in social situations. Still other children tend to be *feisty*. These children are intense, active, distractible, sensitive, moody, and have irregular rhythms. A quick review of Text Box 4.1 can be helpful in identifying your child's and your own typical patterns of response. It is important to understand that children do not necessarily fit into the flexible, fearful, and feisty clusters. Many children show some but not all temperament characteristics in these clusters.

In Chapter 1, we wrote that fathers need to adapt constantly as their children grow and develop. Adapting to a child who is feisty or fearful may be challenging because those children require more attention than flexible children. Feisty children are hard to ignore—they can be loud, emotional, and demanding. Fathers should be aware that there is nothing wrong with feisty or fearful children. The child's temperament is simply the child's unique behavioral style. Fathers may also want to consider the benefits of a feisty personality. Adults who have high-level leadership positions in society are almost always feisty individuals. Company CEOs have gotten where they are because they are smart and feisty. Children who are fearful during early childhood may be more cautious and less likely to engage in risky behaviors. Fathers will want to encourage safe exploration, but they should also appreciate their older child's more cautious approach to potentially dangerous situations. It is also helpful for fathers to consider their own unique temperament and how this interacts with their child's temperament.

Researchers have studied fathers' involvement when they have feisty or fearful children. Geoffrey Brown and his colleagues found that fathers spent less time interacting with temperamentally feisty 2-year-olds than temperamentally easy children.[5] Researchers have also wanted to know if having a feisty child has a negative effect on fathers' relationships with wives or partners. Children's tendency to display negative moods and become easily distressed can be stressful for parents, which can result in higher levels of coparenting conflict, less coparenting support, and lower marital satisfaction. The idea that feisty children can cause father–mother relationship challenges is consistent with the ecological-systems perspective (see Chapter 1), which indicates that stress in one subsystem (father–child relationship) can spill over to other subsystems (father–mother relationship). Fathers who perceive their infants to be feisty tend to report more negative coparenting[6] and lower marital satisfaction.[7] The lesson from this research is that fathers should learn about child temperament and make every effort to understand how their child's temperament affects their interactions with their child and partner. Knowledge about child temperament can help fathers to adapt to their child regardless of their temperament. They should also reflect on their own temperament characteristics and consider how similar they are to their child. This understanding can lead to changing expectations and discovering more effective ways of interacting.

Fathers may sometimes wonder if their child's behavior is developmentally appropriate, or "typical," or is characteristic of a feisty or fearful temperament. It is not always easy to tell the difference between developmentally appropriate behavior and characteristics of temperament. For example, almost all toddlers have temper tantrums and difficulty managing big feelings. These are normal behaviors, but fathers may still wonder if the behaviors are indicative of a "problem." Fathers should speak with a pediatrician or caregiver with years of experience working with young children to get answers to their questions. Here are several reflection questions to help fathers understand child temperament.

## Reflection Questions

♦ How does your child explore the environment? Are they cautious and clinging or do they jump right in?

◆ How easily does your child adapt to change, for example, a change in their routine or schedule?

◆ How does your temperament style differ from your child's? Does this create tension or stress or are your styles compatible?

## Physical Development

Children grow very rapidly during the first three years. They double their weight by age 1 and quadruple their weight by age 2. Gross motor skills—voluntary movements of the large muscle groups (e.g., arms, legs)—develop before fine motor skills. Most infants can hold their heads up, push themselves up, push down on legs, and roll over at ages 4 to 6 months. They can stand holding on and sit with support by 9 months, get to a sitting position and walk holding on to furniture by age 1, walk alone between 12 and 18 months, and run and climb up stairs while holding on by age 2.[8]

Fine motor skills are the small muscle movements of the feet, toes, hands, and fingers. Most children can put things in their mouths by 9 months, bang objects together and reach with one hand by 1 year, eat with a spoon and scribble on paper by 18 months, and build a tower of blocks and draw a straight line and circle by 2 years. Young children develop these skills at different paces based on the interplay of their genetics and environment.

Toddlers are very active and require almost constant attention from parents. Fathers need to assist children in just about everything that they do. They support children when they begin to walk, help them climb stairs, and make sure they are safe when running. Children's gross and fine motor skills mature naturally and are mostly unaffected by parenting practices.[9] However, parents can help children to achieve a sense of mastery by assisting them with activities that are challenging. Parental scaffolding—providing support and modeling problem-solving and learning—helps children gain this sense of mastery. For example, children can become easily frustrated when trying to build a tower or do a simple puzzle. Fathers can help by guiding the child's hand or positioning the toy so the child can complete the task. One of the few studies conducted on fathers' scaffolding showed that fathers are just as effective as mothers in scaffolding and that children were more successful at stacking blocks when fathers engaged in sensitive and contingent scaffolding (assisting the child only when they need help with the toy).[10] Researchers have found that children display better self-regulation (such as delaying eating a snack when told to wait) when mothers assist toddlers with their play contingent on the child's ability and the extent to which the child struggles with the task.[11] There is no reason to expect that fathers will be any less influential than mothers in supporting their young children's development when they use scaffolding strategies.

## Emotional Development

Emotional development is defined as "a gradual increase in the capacity to experience, express, and interpret the full range of emotions and in the ability to cope with them appropriately."[12] Infants begin to express emotions very soon after birth. They cry to express distress when hungry, in pain, sleepy, or frustrated. They smile at approximately 6 weeks. They become still when interested in something, turn away when afraid, slump in posture when sad, and exhibit excitement.[13] Parents influence infants' emotions by expressing emotions themselves, which infants can observe, experience, and begin to imitate.[14] Some parents struggle with their emotions. Parents who experience depression tend to smile less, respond with less excitement to their infants, and are withdrawn. Their infants may also show depressed social behaviors including withdrawal, immobility, and nonresponsiveness to others.

Both mothers and fathers can experience postpartum depression, although it is more common in mothers. According to the Centers for Disease Control, about one in ten women experience postpartum depression—even women who had healthy pregnancies and births.[15] Postpartum depression is different from "the baby blues," which typically disappear a few days after giving birth. Postpartum depression lasts longer and is more intense. Fathers should help the mother seek medical attention if he suspects she has postpartum depression. Fathers can also serve as a buffer to some of the impacts of mothers' depression. The U.S. Office of Women's Health has an excellent website describing the symptoms and treatment for postpartum depression (https://www.womenshealth.gov/mental-health/mental-health-conditions/postpartum-depression).

Fathers' and mothers' emotional availability is critical for children's healthy social–emotional development. Emotional availability includes parents' positive displays of affection and enthusiasm toward the child and low levels of negative displays of hostility, anger, annoyance, or rejection toward the child. Emotional availability also includes sensitivity to the child, that is, baby-centered behavior (e.g., father gauges the infant's interest and mood and paces interactions to fit the infant's cues). In Chapter 3, we indicated that sensitivity is important for developing healthy father–child attachment bonds. Some studies show fathers are less emotionally available to infants than mothers; other studies show no differences.[16] In a study of 1-year-olds, fathers were less emotionally available than mothers, but children showed higher levels of emotional competence when their fathers were emotionally available to them compared with fathers who were not emotionally available.[17] The lessons learned from research are that fathers should make every effort to become emotionally available to their child.

Parents who are emotionally available engage in more emotion talk with children. This is one of the main ways children learn about emotions. Emotion talk involves helping children to be aware of emotions and parents' labeling of their own emotions and children's verbal or nonverbal expressions of emotion. Parents use a wide range of emotion vocabulary when talking to infants and toddlers, including feeling states, such as happy and sad, and desires, such as want and need. Many studies have shown that parents' emotion talk contributes to young children's understanding of emotions[18] and capacity to show empathy.[19] Children are also better able to regulate their own emotions when parents engage in emotion talk. Fathers who engage in emotion talk and respond positively to young children's expressions of emotion are significantly more likely to have children who can regulate their own emotions.[20]

Fathers tend to talk significantly less than mothers about emotions with infants and toddlers.[21] Many men have been socialized to hold in their feelings. Men may have acquired a limited emotion vocabulary. In Chapter 1, we stated that attitudes about masculinity play a significant role in fathers' beliefs and behaviors as parents. Boys and men are often exposed to societal expectations that promote outdated attitudes and behavior about masculinity. These include restricting one's emotions to joy and anger and avoiding the expression of fear and sadness. According to Richard Petts and colleagues, fathers with traditional attitudes about masculinity are significantly less likely to show warmth toward young children.[22] They express less affection and hug and kiss their children less frequently. Being less expressive with children also means using less emotion talk. The Pathways Organization in Chicago offers ways that fathers can support their young children's social–emotional development (see Text Box 4.2).[23] This area of development continues to be a critical focus for developing social–emotional competence during the preschool years and will be addressed again in the Chapter 5.

---

TEXT BOX 4.2

**What You Can Do to Help Your Child's Social-Emotional Development**

◆ **Be a model** of the emotions and behaviors you want your child to show. You are your child's first teacher and they look up to you as a role model.

◆ **Be responsive** to your child's emotions and behaviors. Responding will help to develop trust between you and your child.

◆ **Encourage children** to try new things and learn how much they can do.

Source: Pathways Organization (n.d.), *Social–emotional development.*

## Cognitive Development

Development of cognitive abilities is an important task during infancy and toddlerhood. According to the American Psychological Association, cognitive development is defined as "the growth and maturation of thinking processes of all kinds, including perceiving, remembering, concept formation, problem-solving, imagining, and reasoning."[24] Developmental psychologists suggest that, aside from eating and sleeping, the infant's most important job is to explore the physical and social worlds. A child's mental life starts with development of the senses (seeing, hearing, feeling, tasting) and perceiving their surroundings. The senses are already well-developed at birth. Newborns have very keen hearing and are sensitive to human sounds. They are also sensitive to touch, pain, and taste. Vision is the most poorly developed sense at birth. The sense organs develop rapidly during infancy, but they develop at different times. Touch develops before hearing, which develops before vision. This staggered development allows each sense organ to mature at a high level.[25]

The infant progresses quickly to learning, remembering, and constructing ideas. Children are biologically predisposed to acquire cognitive skills. At first, children learn about the world through direct, physical contact: tasting, feeling, pounding, pushing, hearing, and moving objects in their immediate environment. A few milestones for children of different ages (with some individual differences) include:

- Reach for toys around 4 months
- Bring objects to their mouths around 6 months
- Pick up objects using their thumb and index finger around 9 months
- Bang objects together and put things in a container around 1 year

Infants also learn through reinforcement and modeling. For example, placing a child in a highchair becomes a signal that food is on the way. They also learn when their actions are positively reinforced by parents or others. Jay's 1.5-year-old granddaughter shrieked repeatedly when her older brother laughed and shrieked, too. The older brother reinforced her shrieking by modeling shrieking as a fun activity. Learning also involves imitation. Fathers learn this quickly when their 2-year-old learns a new word after the father slips and says a "bad" word that their toddler repeats over and over.

Research indicates that infants and toddlers have better cognitive skills when fathers are more involved with them.[26] Fathers' interactions with infants as early as the first month following birth (playing, singing, talking, putting to bed, changing diapers, feeding, and soothing) predicted children's cognitive functioning one year later.[27] Infants' cognitive ability at age 9 months (measured as infants' babbling and exploring objects with a purpose) was higher when fathers played, sang, and talked with their infants.[28] .

Jay and his colleagues examined fathers' engagement in cognitively stimulating activities and toddlers' cognitive functioning at age 2.[29] The cognitive skills examined included memory, vocabulary, problem-solving, early counting, and reasoning. Children's skills were higher when fathers were more involved with them. An important finding of this study, and one that supports the ecological-systems perspective, was that fathers' *characteristics* also influenced toddlers' cognition. Specifically, children scored lower on cognitive functioning at age 2 when fathers reported more personal problems (e.g., unemployment, depression, excessive alcohol use, arrests), but only because the man's personal problems negatively affected the mother's interactions with the child. Mothers were less supportive of the child when fathers had many personal problems. This illustrates how fathers can indirectly affect children and demonstrates family system dynamics discussed in Chapter 1. As we wrote there, families are groups of individuals organized into interdependent subsystems. These may include the father–mother, mother–child, father–child, mother–father–child, and sibling subsystems. Jay's research shows how the father–mother subsystem can influence the mother–child subsystem.

## Language Development and Early Literacy

Language acquisition is an important developmental task for infants and toddlers. Newborns communicate with body posture (being relaxed or still), gestures, cries, and facial expressions.[30] A few milestones that occur as they get older include:

- ◆ Babble at approximately 4 months
- ◆ Begin to use consonant sounds and respond to their own name at approximately 6 months
- ◆ Say "mama" and "dada" at approximately 1 year
- ◆ Say several words at approximately 18 months

Infants understand more than they can say. By the time they are 2 years old, they can use about 200 words and speak in short sentences. However, there is wide variation in children's language development. Some children speak several words by 1 year, while other children do not start using words until 18 months or later. The latter group of children usually catch up to their peers who started speaking earlier. Infants' ability to learn language is nothing short of miraculous!

Speaking to children is critical for their development of language. Parents adjust their speech to accommodate the child's ability to hear the sounds and words they are making. They may use a high-pitched voice and exaggerate their facial expressions (baby talk) to get the attention of infants. Infants respond actively to both fathers' and mothers' infant-directed speech and become distressed when parents don't respond to them.[31] Fathers tend to use fewer words and less infant-directed speech than mothers when interacting with children.[32] These differences between fathers and mothers are small. Most studies have not found that fathers' and mothers' talk with infants differs in quality. For example, the complexity of fathers' speech as measured by the length of their utterances seems to be similar to that of mothers.[33] Most importantly, infants' language abilities are positively influenced by fathers' use of infant-directed speech, and there is growing evidence that infants benefit when exposed to multiple speakers.[34]

Infants start to engage in conversation-like exchanges by the end of their second month.[35] Early communication between parents and infants involves taking turns. The infant sets the pace of these interactions, and the parent replies, adjusts, supports, and elaborates on the child's vocalizations. Taking turns has been found to be important for later child development outcomes. Researchers have found that children's initiation of turn-taking communication at age 9 months, followed by fathers' and mothers' responsiveness to the child, was correlated with children's ability to get along with peers at age 4 and their positive social behavior at age 15.[36] Fathers can learn the skill of taking turns in "conversing" with their young children, especially when they understand the importance of this skill for later child development.

It is important to consider fathers' and mothers' preferences for interacting with young children when thinking about children's development. As we saw in Chapters 1 and 3, fathers engage in a lot of play with young children. Fathers' play is frequently more stimulating, vigorous, and arousing than mothers' play. These interaction styles promote the child's risk-taking and exploration,[37] which in turn facilitates the development of cognitive skills.[38] In addition, fathers' play introduces children to vocabulary that mothers may not use. Jay talks to his 2-year-old granddaughter about rockets. She has even learned the word "gravity" as a result of these interactions, even though she won't understand the concept for a long time.

One aspect of early literacy and language development that is strongly related to later school success is book reading by parents.[39] The specific benefits of fathers' book reading are not as well understood as the benefits of mothers' book reading.[40] Reading to infants as early as 4 months is recommended by Zero to Three (2019) as advice to parents.[41] The benefits of reading by fathers include different styles of reading that provide more variety. Fathers can serve as role models for the importance of reading. Reading together with infants and toddlers also helps fathers and children feel physically and emotionally close and strengthens the father–child relationship. Fathers read most frequently to their children who are ages 1 to 4.[42] Early reading has a positive impact on language development.[43] In addition to book reading, talking to children, singing together, and telling stories support early language and literacy development and brings fathers and their infants and toddlers closer.

## Summary

Fathers occupy an important role in their infants' and toddlers' development. We know now that children's development is positively affected when fathers are engaged in all aspects of caregiving with their young children (including play), when they are sensitive and responsive to their cues, emotionally available, communicative about feelings, and engaged in cognitive stimulation. Importantly, research has increasingly demonstrated that fathers have positive effects on children above and beyond the effects of mothers. Most past studies have focused on fathers and mothers who live together, but there is a growing body of research on fathers who do not reside with children. In coming years, we should know more about how nonresident fathers affect child development. Because fathers play an important role in child development, it is essential for fathers to learn how infants and toddlers develop. This chapter shows that there is much to be learned. The transition to becoming a new father is a time of significant change for men. Fathers are likely to find the transition more rewarding and have a more positive impact on their families when they understand infant and toddler development.

## Notes

1 National Safety Council. (2021). *Deaths by demographics: Age and cause.* injuryfacts.nsc.org/all-injuries/deaths-by-demographics/deaths-by-age/data-details/

2 Schwebel, D. C., & Brezausek, C. M. (2004). The role of fathers in toddlers' unintentional injury risk. *Journal of Pediatric Psychology, 29*(10), 19–28. https://doi.org/10.1093/jpepsy/jsh003

3 National Center for Fathering. (n.d.). *Dads and childproofing.* http://fathers.com/blog/your-kids/preschoolers/dads-and-childproofing/

4 Chess, S., & Thomas, A. (2016). *Temperament (Basic principles into practice)* (1st ed.). Routledge.
5 Brown, G. L., McBride, B. A., Bost, K. K., & Shin, N. (2011). Parental involvement, child temperament, and parents' work hours: Differential relations for mothers and fathers. *Journal of Applied Developmental Psychology, 32*(6), 313–322. https://doi.org/10.1016/j.appdev.2011.08.004
6 Burney, R. V., & Leerkes, E. M. (2010). Links between mothers' and fathers' perceptions of infant temperament and coparenting. *Infant Behavior and Development, 33*(2), 125–135. https://doi.org/10.1016/j.infbeh.2009.12.002; Gordon, I., & Feldman, R. (2008). Synchrony in the triad: A microlevel process model of coparenting and parent–child interactions. *Family Process, 47*(4), 465–479. https://doi.org/10.1111/j.1545-5300.2008.00266.x
7 Mehall, K. G., Spinrad, T. L., Eisenberg, N., & Gaertner, B. M. (2009). Examining the relations of infant temperament and couples' marital satisfaction to mother and father involvement: A longitudinal study. *Fathering, 7*(1), 23–48. https://doi.org/10.3149/fth.0701.23
8 Paris, J., Ricardo, A., & Rymond, D. (2019). *Child growth and development.* College of the Canyons. https://open.umn.edu/opentextbooks/textbooks/750
9 Gesell, A. (2014). *Infant and child in the culture of today.* Harper & Row.
10 Conner, D. B., Knight, D. K., & Cross, D. R. (1997). Mothers' and fathers' scaffolding of their 2-year-olds during problem-solving and literacy interactions. *British Journal of Developmental Psychology, 15*, 323–338. https://doi.org/10.1111/j.2044-835X.1997.tb00524.x
11 Neale, D., & Whitebread, D. (2019). Maternal scaffolding during play with 12- to 24-month-old infants: Stability over time and relations with emerging effortful control. *Metacognition Learning, 14*, 265–289. https://doi.org/10.1007/s11409-019-09196-6
12 American Psychological Association. (n.d.). *Emotional development.* http://dictionary.apa.org/emotional development
13 Bornstein, M. H., & Arterberry, M. E. (2022). *Infancy: The basics.* Routledge.
14 Bornstein, M. H., & Arterberry, M. E. (2022). *Infancy.*
15 Centers for Disease Control and Prevention. (n.d.). *Postpartum depression.* www.cdc.gov/reproductivehealth/depression/index.htm#Postpartum
16 Bergmann, S., & Klein, A. M. (2020). Fathers' emotional availability with their children: Determinants and consequences. In H. E. Fitzgerald, K. von Klitzing, N. J. Cabrera, J. Scarano de Mendonça, & T. Skjøthaug (Eds.), *Handbook of fathers and child development.* Springer.
17 Volling, B. L., McElwain, N. L., Notaro, P. C., & Herrera, C. (2002). Parents' emotional availability and infant emotional competence: Predictors of parent–infant attachment and emerging self-regulation. *Journal of Family Psychology, 16*(4), 447–465. https://doi.org/10.1037/0893-3200.16.4.447
18 Ensor, R., & Hughes, C. (2008). Content or connectedness? Mother–child talk and early social understanding. *Child Development, 79*, 201–216. https://doi.org/10.1111/j.1467-8624.2007.01120.x
19 Drummond, J., Paul, E. F., Waugh, W. E., Hammond, S. I., & Brownell, C. A. (2014). Here, there and everywhere: Emotion and mental state talk in different social contexts predicts empathic helping in toddlers. *Frontiers in Psychology, 5*(361). https://doi.org/10.3389/fpsyg.2014.00361
20 Islamiah, N., Breinholst, S., Walczak, M. A., & Esbjørn, B. H. (2023). The role of fathers in children's emotion regulation development: A systematic review. *Infant and Child Development, 32*(2), e2397. https://doi.org/10.1002/icd.2397

21 Zaman, W., & Fivush, R. (2013). Gender differences in elaborative parent–child emotion and play narratives. *Sex Roles, 68*, 591–604. https://doi.org/10.1007/s11199-013-0270-7

22 Petts, R. J., Shafer, K. M., & Essig, L. (2018). Does adherence to masculine norms shape fathering behavior?: Masculinity and father involvement. *Journal of Marriage and Family, 80*(3), 704–720. https://doi.org/10.1111/jomf.12476

23 Pathways Organization. (n.d.). *Social–emotional development.* https://pathways.org/topics-of-development/social-emotional/

24 American Psychological Association. (n.d.). *Cognitive development.* http://dictionary.apa.org/cognitive-development

25 Bornstein, M. H., & Arterberry, M. E. (2022). *Infancy.*

26 Tamis-LeMonda, C. S., Shannon, J. D., Cabrera, N. J., & Lamb, M. E. (2004). Fathers and mothers at play with their 2- and 3-year-olds: Contributions to language and cognitive development. *Child Development, 75*(6), 1806–1820. https://doi.org/10.1111/j.1467-8624.2004.00818.x

27 Nugent, J. K. (1991). Cultural and psychological influences on the father's role in infant development. *Journal of Marriage and the Family, 53*(2), 475–485. https://doi.org/10.2307/352913

28 Bronte-Tinkew, J., Carrano, J., Horowitz, A., & Kinukawa, A. (2008). Involvement among resident fathers and links to infant cognitive outcomes. *Journal of Family Issues, 29*(9), 1211–1244. https://doi.org/10.1177/0192513X08318145

29 Cabrera, N., Fagan, J., Wight, V., & Schadler, C. (2011). The influence of mother, father, and child risk on parenting and children's cognitive and social behaviors. *Child Development, 82*,1985–2005. https://doi.org/10.1111/j.1467-8624.2011.01667.x

30 Paris, J., Ricardo, A., & Rymond, D. (2019). *Child growth and development.*

31 Saliba, S., Gratier, M., Filippa, M., Devouche, E., & Esseily, R. (2020). Fathers' and mothers' infant directed speech influences preterm infant behavioral state in the NICU. *Journal of Nonverbal Behavior, 44*, 437–451. https://doi.org/10.1007/s10919-020-00335-1

32 Shapiro, N. T., Hippe, D., & Ferjan Ramirez, N. (2021). How chatty are daddies? An exploratory study of infants' language environment. *Journal of Speech, Language, and Hearing Research, 64*(8), 3242–3252. https://doi.org/10.1044/2021_JSLHR-20-00727

33 Ramírez, F. N. (2022). Fathers' infant-directed speech and its effects on child language development. *Language & Linguistics Compass*, e12448. https://doi.org/10.1111/lnc3.12448

34 Ramírez, F. N. (2022). Fathers' infant-directed speech; Shapiro, N. T., Hippe, D., & Ferjan Ramirez, N. (2021). How chatty are daddies?

35 Gratier, M., Devouche, E., Guellai, B., Infanti, R., Yilmaz, E., & Parlato-Oliveira, E. (2015). Early development of turn-taking in vocal interaction between mothers and infants. *Frontiers in Psychology, 6*, 1167. https://doi.org/ 10.3389/fpsyg.2015.01167

36 Hedenbro, M., & Rydelius, P.-A. (2018). Children's abilities to communicate with both parents in infancy were related to their social competence at the age of 15. *Acta Paediatrica, 108*, 118–123. https://doi.org/10.1111/apa.14430

37 Kromelow, S., Harding, C., & Touris, M. (1990). The role of the father in the development of stranger sociability during the second year. *American Journal of Orthopsychiatry, 60*(4), 521–530. https://doi.org/10.1037/h0079202

38 Sethna, V., Perry, E., Domoney, J., Iles, J., Psychogiou, L., Rowbotham, N. E. L., Stein, A., Murray, L., & Ramchandani, P. G. (2017). Father–child

interactions at 3 months and 24 months: Contributions to children's cognitive development at 24 months. *Infant Mental Health Journal, 38,* 378–390. https://doi.org/10.1002/imhj.21642

39  Whitehurst, G. J., Falco, F. L., Lonigan, C. J., Fischel, J. E., DeBaryshe, B. D., Valdez-Menchaca, M. C., & Caulfield, M. (1988). Accelerating language development through picture book reading. *Developmental Psychology, 24,* 552–559. https://doi.org/10.1037/0012-1649.24.4.552; Neuman, S., & Dickinson, D. (Eds.). (2003). *Handbook of family literacy research.* Guilford Press.

40  Pancsofar, N., & Vernon-Feagans, L. (2006). Mother and father language input to young children: Contributions to later language development. *Journal of Applied Developmental Psychology, 27*(6), 571–587.https://doi.org/10.1016/j.appdev.2006.08.003

41  Zero to Three. (2019). *Read early and often.* www.zerotothree.org/resource/read-early-and-often/#:~:text=Reading%20together%20when%20babies%20are,even%20before%20he%20can%20talk!

42  Palm, G. (2013). Fathers and early literacy. In J. Pattnaik (Ed.), *Father involvement in young children's lives* (pp. 13–30). Springer.

43  Quach, J., Sarkadi, A., Napiza, N., Wake, M., Lourhman, A., & Goldfeld, S. (2018). Do fathers' home reading practices at age 2 predict language and literacy at age 4? *Academic Pediatrics, 18*(2), 179–187. https://doi.org/10.1016/j.acap.2017.10.001

# 5

# Fathers and Preschoolers

## Play, Curiosity, and Endless Energy

*I enjoy being able to experience many firsts, like reading to them and they appreciate the story. They make their own art projects independently. I get to be along for their discoveries of the world. They aren't big kids and they need a lot of guidance. There is also backsliding—like potty training—and this can be frustrating. As a person, being a father has made me think about what I value and how I spend my time.*

—Father of a 3-year-old son and a 5-year-old
daughter

## Introduction

"Early childhood" refers to the stage of development for children ages 3 through 5. Children make significant changes during these years in the way they look, express and regulate their emotions, think, communicate, and interact with peers, adults, and the world. Preschoolers love to play and spend many hours doing so. Physical growth during this time begins to slow down while brain development is at its peak from ages 0 to 5.[1] At age 1, children recognize about 50 words; by age 3, they recognize about 1,000 words; and by age 5, they recognize at least 10,000 words.[2] Social, emotional, and creative skills also develop rapidly during this time.[3] Preschoolers begin to assert their independence and test the limits established by parents.

Fathers often become more involved in their child's lives during this stage of development. Fathers' contributions to the

DOI: 10.4324/9781003486107-5

development of their preschool children are many and varied. As more fathers become involved with their children during this time, research shows evidence of great benefits for children across multiple developmental domains.[4] It can also be a stressful time for fathers when both parents work and have to manage childcare arrangements. During this stage of development, fathers decide what kind of authority figure they want to be and what parenting style they will adopt.[5]

In earlier American history, fathers were seen primarily as moral guides for their children.[6] This role changed over time and the breadwinner role took precedence along with the disciplinarian role, which often was turned into the "enforcer." "Wait until your father gets home" was a familiar threat for children growing up in latter half of the twentieth century. As expectations for fathers' involvement changed, as noted in Chapter 1, fathers of young children assumed the roles of caregiver, playmate, coach, and teacher, as well as disciplinarian, provider, and moral guide.

This chapter begins with a focus on the developmental tasks of fathers during the preschool years. The second section focuses on the central role of play in supporting development and the unique role of play in connecting fathers and children. The third section describes important developmental tasks of children during the preschool years. These tasks explain a preschool child's motivations as they interact with their family and the larger world. The different domains of physical, cognitive, emotional, and social development are interconnected as children approach developmental tasks. The child begins to construct their understanding of self during the preschool years. Finally, the chapter will address challenges that contemporary fathers face: finding and sharing childcare, managing screen time, and addressing a child's special needs that may emerge during the preschool years.

## Developmental Tasks of Fathers during the Preschool Years

Ellen Galinsky identified three developmental tasks that fathers face as their children enter the preschool years and move out into the world.[7] First, is the socialization of children, that is, helping them understand the social rules and norms in the family and larger society. This is a time for fathers to consider the morals and values that they want to pass on to their children. A second task for fathers during this period is deciding how to express authority and set boundaries on child behavior. The third task for fathers is negotiating new coparenting challenges as parents work through differences in parenting practices, sharing family responsibilities, and creating family routines and traditions that reflect shared family values. Parents who live together, as well as parents in separate households, find ways to work together in managing different child-rearing beliefs and practices.

## Socialization: Defining Values and Expectations for Children

Parents are the first and most important teachers of their young children; they play a crucial role in preparing their young children for entry into school and larger society. The "teacher" label is often interpreted to mean that parents need to teach their young children early academic skills (e.g., colors, letters, and numbers). This knowledge is important to help children prepare for school and formal learning. However, the more important curriculum involves the values and social–emotional learning that parents teach their children primarily through their actions and reactions. Fathers of young children are mostly focused on immediate issues, such as dealing with a fussy eater, a child not sleeping at night, toilet training, managing tantrums, curiosity about their body, getting along with peers, and how much screen time they are allowed. These immediate concerns should be considered in the context of the underlying values and messages that fathers want to teach their child. These values may be clearly defined by fathers based on their religious beliefs, their culture, and their family of origin.

As a parent educator, Glen helps fathers consider and identify the important values that they want to teach their children. These provide a foundation for thinking about day-to-day issues in the context of long-term outcomes. There are times when fathers choose to define their own moral values as different from those they grew up with. Glen asks fathers on the first day of class to introduce themselves and their child(ren) and share the most important lesson that they want to pass on to their children. He hears a variety of responses from respecting others, being a leader, and working hard to being honest and kind. It is important for fathers to take time to reflect on the underlying values that they want their children to learn. Clarity about underlying values also informs what kinds of expectations and goals fathers have for children. Parenting styles and practices are most effective when they are consistent with these values. This is also a time when family routines and traditions are established. This helps children to understand expectations and learn family values as they celebrate family traditions together.

## Fathers as Authority Figures

Children's new skills and expressions of independence as they move out into the world starting at ages 2.5 through 3 push fathers to adjust their parenting practices. This is an important time for fathers to find a balance between setting limits and expressing love and care for their young children, who are expressing their independence by testing limits. The research on parenting styles is well-established and describes three different combinations of parenting practices based on two dimensions—parental support and parental control.[8] The three parenting styles were originally identified as authoritative, authoritarian, and permissive by Diana Baumrind.[9] Farzana Bibi and colleagues have described these different styles and their related impacts on child outcomes:[10]

◆ Authoritative parents balance their demands with responsiveness. They hold reasonable expectations for children and set firm limits. At the same time, they are warm and understanding of their children and engage them in problem-solving and decision-making.
◆ Authoritarian parents focus on parent control and are demanding. They are not as responsive to children's needs nor understanding of their perspective. They assert

their power and use physical and psychological control techniques (e.g., threats, physical force, and withdrawal of approval). They set high standards and expect children to be obedient.

◆ Permissive parents have few clear or predictable rules and tend to be less consistent with consequences. They are nurturing and accepting and give children a great deal of freedom.

These three styles have been identified in research on parenting as having predictable outcomes for children.[11] Authoritative parents are more likely to have children who demonstrate greater success in school and are well-adjusted. Parents with authoritarian and permissive styles have children who display more internalizing (anxiety and depression) and externalizing (acting out and aggression) behaviors.[12]

The idea of developing a parenting style around the dimensions of control and expressions of warmth leads to discussions about discipline and punishment in parenting classes. In Glen's exploration of physical punishment with incarcerated fathers, he asks men about the forms of discipline that were used when they were children. Physical punishment has been a common theme. The men described the various ways that they were hit by their parents and the different items that were used. These were often whatever was handy—belts, switches, electrical cords, hairbrushes—and reflected abusive behavior. The responses over 25 years have shifted to less use of physical punishment by parents and more time outs or taking away privileges. This coincides with a study of 35-year-old parents from 1993–2017 that reported a decline from 50% to 35% of parents who reported spanking their children.[13] Most of the incarcerated fathers do not want to use physical punishment with their children, but they often have no role models and are uncertain about how to assert their authority and set limits in a positive way.

Child abuse laws in their current form in the United States were passed beginning in the early 1970s. The introduction of child abuse laws created uncertainty about whether parents could or should use physical punishment as a regular form of discipline. Spanking was a common form of punishment in the United States during the 1950s and 1960s. It has taken a couple of generations for new parenting attitudes and behaviors to emerge. Laws led to changes in parenting attitudes and behaviors, while educators introduced new strategies and practices to help parents feel comfortable in disciplining their children. Fathers often look to their own fathers as role models, and even if they don't want to be like their fathers, it takes effort to learn new strategies.

There continues to be tension about the best ways to teach children social norms. The research on parenting styles across time and cultures has consistently pointed out the negative impacts of the authoritarian parenting style that often uses physical punishment as a primary way to assert control.[14] This leads both fathers and mothers to search for alternative ways to teach children and respond to child misbehaviors. A model that Glen has found useful for parents who feel that taking away spanking leaves them feeling powerless is to introduce a parenting "toolbox." The toolbox includes three components: *nurturance* (use humor, tell stories, provide routines), *guidance* (show child how to do something, redirect, say firm "no"), and *consequence strategies* (time out, lose a privilege, natural consequences). See Text Box 5.1 for selected examples of strategies in each of the three areas. This framework was adapted from a University of Minnesota Extension Service parenting curriculum that was developed in the 1990s.[15] Glen uses this framework to help parents see that there are many different commonsense approaches that can be used to nurture, teach, and guide children. The model depends upon building a relationship based on nurturance (the warmth dimension), guidance (teaching strategies), and consequences (control) that can be used to enforce rules. In developing a parenting style, a general principle reflected in the authoritative style is a balance of warmth and control. The toolbox provides parents with a number of possible choices and strategies for developing a warm, supportive relationship and guiding children towards positive social behavior and emotional regulation.

---

**TEXT BOX 5.1**

**Parenting Toolbox—Sample Strategies**

**Nurturance and Prevention**—Strategies to show care, nurture, and prevent problems

---

- Help child to manage change
- See child's point of view
- Show affection
- Use humor
- Change the activity
- Spend time together
- Encourage humor and fun
- Provide routines
- Listen carefully
- Distract or redirect
- Prepare child for difficulty
- Tell stories to teach values

---

**Teaching and Guidance**—Strategies to manage conflict and teach responsibility

---

- Be clear about rules
- Offer substitutes
- Say a firm "no"
- Show child how
- Seek support or advice from a friend
- Compromise with child
- Acknowledge and accept child's feelings
- Take a break
- Ask child for solutions

---

**Consequence Tools**—Strategies when other tools don't work and child misbehaves

---

- Remove child from activity
- Express strong disappointment
- Use a time out
- Take away privileges

---

Take time to reflect on some of the items in Text Box 5.1 that you use or would like to try with your young child. It provides some simple alternatives to physical punishment. It also emphasizes the importance of taking time to focus on building a secure relationship as part of the long-term strategy for teaching children.

The following questions may be helpful in exploring your parenting style. First consider what parenting styles were used by your parents and how they influence you individually and your relationship with your parents.

## Reflection Questions

- ◆ What kinds of discipline were used by your father? By your mother?
- ◆ How did you feel about the way your mother and father disciplined you?
- ◆ How do you want to be the same or different?
- ◆ How do you want to balance control and warmth?
- ◆ What is your child's temperament and how do they respond to your parenting style?

## Areas of Tension between Coparents

The importance of a positive coparenting relationship begins during prenatal development (see Chapter 2). Coparenting patterns about sharing parenting responsibilities solidify during the first year. The preschool years introduce some new parenting practices for fathers and mothers to negotiate. What manners do they want to teach their child? What child behaviors are not acceptable? Parents often have different answers to these questions. One of the developmental tasks for parents during this stage is to address the important areas of tension around raising children, including how parents approach discipline as part of their parenting style. Both parents also have to negotiate how to manage work–family balance and how to share household and childcare responsibilities.

Yosi Yaffee, in a review of studies from 15 different countries, found that fathers tend to be more authoritarian in style, while mothers are more authoritative.[16] Mothers were more accepting, responsive, and supportive and gave the child more autonomy than fathers. In Glen's work as a parent educator with fathers, he frequently hears that mothers are too soft on children. Fathers say that the children listen better to them and they feel that they are more effective in setting and enforcing limits than mothers. Fathers' larger size and deeper voices often give them an advantage in gaining compliance from young children. Behind this short-term obedience, however, is sometimes a child's fear of a father who may be large, loud, and imposing. Fear can have a negative impact on the child and the father–child relationship.

Tanya Tavassolie and her colleagues discuss the associations between different maternal and paternal parenting styles and marital conflict (such as arguments).[17] Marital conflict increased when mothers saw themselves as more authoritative and fathers as more authoritarian. Outcomes for children were better when fathers saw themselves as more permissive than mothers and mothers as more authoritarian than fathers. Fathers and mothers should work together to discuss differences in parenting styles. Most fathers (and mothers) do not want to fall into the role of always being the disciplinarian or "bad cop," which can get in the way of having a close relationship with their children. Preschool years are a time to reflect on how different parenting styles impact both the mother–father relationship and the father–child relationship.

As mothers and fathers have moved towards more equal sharing of childcare responsibilities, some of the issues that have emerged can be characterized as gender tensions. Mothers feel that men don't listen and do not show feelings. Mothers talk about having an endless list of things to do with never enough time. Fathers can feel left out and sometimes guilty for not doing enough. As parents aspire to be equal coparents, these are typical feelings that parents have to negotiate.

These developmental tasks can be reframed as opportunities for men to grow and develop. Young children help fathers to consider what is most important in life. As fathers learn new ways to connect with and guide their preschool children, they learn new skills, such as being more open with feelings and more sensitive to coparents' feelings and needs. Coparenting tensions can cause parents to move further apart or closer together. Parents can learn new conflict resolution skills and discover parenting practices that reflect their values and goals for their children. This will bring them closer together and help children know what to expect from their parents.

## Learning through Play: Father–Child Connection during Preschool Years

Play has an important role in preschoolers' learning. The intersection of fathers' style of play and the value of play for development is a "sweet spot" that supports growth in both father and child. Glen witnessed this intersection of fathers and preschool children during Super Saturdays, a program for dads and preschool children that started in 1984 and continues to the present. Fathers bring their children to the Saturday morning class, where they get to play together. Some weeks they play games in the gym or they cook and prepare snacks together. Other weeks they create art projects or work on simple science projects or building activities. The children are excited to be there and have the undisturbed attention of their fathers.[18]

Play is the primary way that children learn during preschool years.[19] An extensive review of research on play and learning (more than 300 studies) was conducted by the Lego Foundation.[20] Most of these studies focused on young children ages 3–5. Play promotes skill development in multiple developmental domains, including:

◆ Cognitive (concentration, problem-solving, and flexible thinking)
◆ Emotional (understanding, managing, and expressing emotions)
◆ Social (collaborating and communicating, understanding others' perspectives)
◆ Physical (fine and gross motor skills)
◆ Creative (new ideas and associations)

The frequency of father–child play increases as children move from infancy to preschool and then declines as they move into middle childhood.[21] Natasha Cabrera and Lori Roggman describe fathers' play style: "Fathers play more playfully—with more humor and spontaneity, and the quality of their play tends to be more physical and boisterous."[22] Both the father–child relationship and child learning and development can be enriched when they take the time to play together.

In a review of fathers and play interactions, eight different types of play activities were identified, including creative, free, locomotor, rough and tumble, video game, puzzle, toy, and combined forms of play.[23] The many ways that fathers and children play together are connected to positive outcomes for children. For example, rough and tumble play with fathers has been related to promoting gross motor skills, emotional regulation, and executive function skills.[24] Executive functioning refers to the conscious control of thought and action, goal-directed responses, and self-regulatory ability.[25] These skills are important for later academic success.[26] The different types of play create multiple opportunities for fathers to promote child growth and development and have fun together.

Five characteristics of play have been found to impact learning[27] (see Text Box 5.2). These characteristics interface with what research says about qualities of fathers' play with children. When fathers are attuned to a child's needs, understand what is meaningful, are involved in back-and-forth interaction, and share positive emotion in their play, they support development of multiple skills and growth in their children.[28]

---

**TEXT BOX 5.2**

**Characteristics of Playful Learning**

1. **Actively engaging**—Children participate in fun activities while discovering new ideas
2. **Meaningful**—Children learn when they connect with content they care about and make connections to what they already know
3. **Social**—Children learn from social interaction and communicating with others
4. **Iterative**—Children actively explore, repeat, vary experiences, and test ideas about how the world works
5. **Joyful**—Children are excited about learning something new or trying out new solutions

---

The type of father–child play that has been studied in most depth is rough and tumble play. One of the areas that has been studied is the impact of rough and tumble play on self-regulation. In Chapter 3 we described how this type of play allows fathers and children to have fun together while also setting limits and teaching children how to calm down when play becomes too wild. Fathers who engage in rough and tumble play without providing consistent boundaries may have a negative influence on children that is related to increased aggression and problems with emotional regulation. The father's role is to engage in play that is challenging but not overly stimulating and that helps children to learn the limits of what is safe and fun. This type of play also improves a child's executive function.[29]

There is a continuum of play with preschool children that starts with free play when the child is in control. At the other end is direct instruction where the adult has total control. In the middle of the continuum is guided play,[30] which allows children to lead the play with adult interaction and guidance. Playing games is also part of the continuum. Games are more adult-directed with established rules, although rules can be made up or modified. Glen experienced this with his 7-year-old grandson while playing a game of Harry Potter Uno. Grandson Hugo decided to introduce a new rule that allowed for more cards to be played in a single turn. It moved the game along more quickly. Hugo felt empowered to be able to create and try out a new rule.

The interactions along the continuum of play involve different roles for fathers.

◆ During *free play*, fathers can follow the child's lead in make-believe play and be a *playmate*. This is an opportunity for fathers to be an *observer* and to better understand a child's interests and ways of thinking. Fathers can also be a *colearner* in exploring the outdoors, sharing observations and information about plants and other natural features, and sharing wonder and curiosity about nature.

◆ During *guided play*, fathers can ask questions to engage the child's problem-solving skills.

◆ While *playing games*, fathers can *model* how to follow rules and have fun even when losing a game. Learning how to follow rules and play games provides a great opportunity to develop social, emotional, and problem-solving skills.

◆ During *direct instruction*, fathers initiate and direct a learning activity involving specific skills. For example, a father can provide materials for his 5-year-old child to create a birthday card for a friend and help with thinking about what to say and how to spell the greeting.

The research on both playful learning and father involvement clearly reports the central role of high-quality interactions.[31] It is essential for fathers to be attuned to a child's needs and interests, bring a sense of playfulness, and engage in back-and-forth interactions that can include asking questions and providing support, structure, and limits when needed. Not all father–child play is positive. Fathers can be too controlling and criticize or interfere with play.[32] Preschool years are a time to bring together father's playful tendencies and children's propensity to learn through play to promote a positive father–child relationship and enhance child learning. Here are several self-reflection questions to help fathers reflect about their play with their child.

### Reflections Questions
  ◆ What are the types of play that your child enjoys with you?
  ◆ What types of play are you most comfortable with?
  ◆ What are the strengths that you bring to playful learning interactions with your child?
  ◆ What roles do you enjoy most when playing with your child?
  ◆ What kinds of play bring you both joy and a feeling of accomplishment?

## Understanding Development in Preschool Children

Children between the ages of 3 and 6 continue to develop and learn at a rapid pace even though physical development (including brain development) has slowed from the earlier pace during ages 0–3. They move from the self-centered toddler years to a greater understanding of self and the world.[33] Two important themes drive development during this stage. The first is the development of the child's identity as a separate, unique person. The second is the development of the child's sense of power and agency in the world as they begin to move beyond the family. As fathers understand typical developmental patterns, they can form realistic expectations for child behavior. They can also find new pathways for giving support and guidance as children take another step out into the larger world.

## Physical Development

Preschool children become more capable of learning new small and large motor skills during this stage. They can turn pages in a book, build taller towers, and use different instruments for drawing and writing. A few milestones include:

♦ They draw pictures of people by age 5 with six body parts.
♦ They begin to draw circles by age 3 that turn into capital letters by age 4 and can print both numbers and letters by age 5.[34]
♦ When they go outside at age 3, they like to run and learn to pedal a tricycle.
♦ At age 4 they begin to hop and are better at catching a bounced ball.
♦ They learn to skip and do somersaults by the time they are 5.

Preschoolers love to go to the park to swing, slide, and climb. They love it when you not only watch while they try something new but also interact with them while they are playing.

**Physical Activity and Health.** Fathers are important role models for young children who observe their eating and exercise habits. Research suggests that diet quality and physical activity are important factors related to child obesity. Rachel Vollmer and her colleagues found that fathers' body fat mass (BMI), diet, and physical activity are significantly associated with their preschool-age children's BMI, diet, and physical activity.[35] This type of finding suggests that fathers can be an important factor in preventing obesity in young children. Morgan and colleagues in Australia recruited 125 fathers and their preschool children (ages

3–5) to participate in an eight-week program to increase their physical activity.[36] The results of the study showed that children participating in the program increased their daily activity levels; this increase continued when assessed nine months later. This demonstrates the importance of engaging fathers in programs to improve family health habits.

**Toilet Training.** The process of toilet training young children is one of the least pleasant tasks for most parents. One of the challenges is to understand this as a long-term process with many different steps for children to become totally independent with toileting and staying dry at night. Gwen Dewar took a careful look at the science behind toilet-training practices.[37] There are some cultures where toilet training begins before 12 months. This is the typical practice in China, where parents learn child's elimination cues and babies then learn parent signals to trigger elimination. The research there suggests that children can learn elimination control early, which has some health benefits, such as fewer diaper rashes and related infections.

Training in the United States typically starts between 18 months to 3 years. Parents tend to let children take the lead. They look for signs that a child might be ready, for example, when they stay dry for longer periods of time and begin to notice and are uncomfortable with wet or soiled clothing. One of the disadvantages of starting too early is that it may take longer and involve more mistakes that can be frustrating for both father and child. Successful learning occurs when children have transitioned to wearing underwear with just a few accidents a week. Children still need fathers' assistance and reminders. It may take longer for children to stay dry at night and accidents may still occur until ages 6–7. There is no specific research on fathers' role in toilet training, but some basic tips apply—be aware of signs of readiness, expect mistakes, and don't punish children for their mistakes.

**Sexual Development.** This is a topic that can be difficult for fathers, but young children's curiosity about their bodies and the bodies of others makes sexual development hard to ignore. The typical response Glen hears from fathers when bringing up their role as sex educators is that it doesn't need to happen until the children are preteens. On the contrary, researchers note that the transmission of values about sexuality from parents to children is inevitable and starts in early childhood.[38] They also found that both fathers and mothers want to be involved in teaching their children about sexuality but often fall short of their aspirations.

Understanding typical sexual behaviors in young children is important to being an effective sex educator. The American Academy of Pediatrics Council on Child Abuse and Neglect identifies a number of common sexual behaviors for 2–6-year-olds that include touching genitals in public or private, viewing or touching peers' or siblings' genitals, and trying to view peers or adults naked.[39] Kent Chrisman and Donna Couchenour describe preschool children's curiosity about body parts and gender differences as a natural part of sexuality development.[40] Preschool children do not think about sexuality as adults do and are inherently sensual and curious about body differences among children born as girls and children born as boys. They masturbate unless taught not to, enjoy bathroom humor, and are curious about where babies come from.

Both fathers and mothers encounter these issues in preschool children and have to decide what values around sexuality they want to promote and how best to respond to questions and behavior. Parents must decide what to teach their children about healthy sexuality and they must decide on the limits for sexual behavior and exploration. This may include giving proper names to body parts and talking about what kinds of touching are okay or not okay. Families also get to decide family rules about modesty and privacy. This sounds easy but as the research suggests, parents are often not comfortable talking about sexuality directly with young children. When having the discussion about sexuality with a group of fathers of young children, Glen posed the question "What is healthy male sexuality?" and the group laughed. They were embarrassed and also realized that this is not an easy question to answer. The American Academy of Pediatrics Council on Child Abuse and Neglect provides some practical guidelines for teaching your preschool child about sexuality (see Text Box 5.3).[41]

> **TEXT BOX 5.3**
>
> **Parents as Sex Educators with Young Children**
>
> 1. Parents should have a discussion about their values and how they want their children to think and feel about their bodies.
> 2. Reflect on your own experience as a child, how your parents managed this role, and the impact it has had on you. Do you want to be different from your parents? In what ways?
> 3. Decide on the names that you want to use for body parts and what toilet language is acceptable in your family.
> 4. Consider your family's ways of respecting privacy and how to teach your child about modesty.
> 5. Help your child understand okay and not-okay touch.
> 6. Media, from TV to billboards, is filled with messages about sexuality. How do you want to control and discuss this in your family?
> 7. Children will ask questions. Be prepared to answer them in simple and direct ways that they can understand that reflect your values.
>
> Source: American Academy of
> Pediatrics Council on Child Abuse and Neglect (2023).

Fathers may want to consider taking a parenting class where they can discuss this area of development with other parents. Parenting classes can be helpful to clarify one's own attitudes and values about sexual behavior among preschoolers. Pediatricians or family doctors can also be helpful in addressing issues around young children's curiosity and normal behavior around sexuality.

## Social Development

The preschool years are a critical time for children to learn new social skills as they take steps beyond the family and interact with peers. They are moving from a self-centered understanding to being able to understand the perspective of others. They begin to understand how others think and to develop a sense of empathy.

Prosocial skills involve learning to share, help, and comfort others. Both authoritative and permissive parenting styles promote prosocial behaviors.[42] Children who are securely attached to their parents—who are sensitive and responsive to a child's needs and support exploration—also tend to be more prosocial. Children's attachment and involvement with fathers are also associated with preschool children's prosocial behavior.[43] Fathers model caring and sharing through their interactions at home, such as responding to family members and sharing household and childcare tasks.

Children also develop social skills through their interactions with peers at playdates, childcare, or early education programs and with siblings or cousins. Their play becomes more sophisticated, and they move from parallel play next to someone doing a similar activity to cooperative play with other preschool children. They may create specific roles, such as superheroes or roles that mimic adults. They learn to share ideas and resolve differences while they play together. This can be a fun time to observe children and provide guidance to help children think about how to solve problems and manage conflicts.

Fathers are often seen as a connection to the larger social world as they bring a young child along to the supermarket, hardware store, or on other errands. Fathers can also help teach young children about respect for others and manners during these trips into the community.[44] Children watch how their parents interact with others and want to emulate the positive behaviors they see when their fathers help someone in the parking lot or thank a store employee for telling them where to find an item. Fathers can also take their young children to the library, park, zoo, or museum as a simple way to introduce them to the community and teach them social graces and norms in different settings.

## Cognitive Development

Preschool-age children grow in many ways as they work to make sense of the world.[45] They try to figure out how everything in their environment works. They begin to understand causality by observing the natural world, such as learning about the wind when they walk out on an autumn day and observe the leaves blowing around and falling from trees. They are full of "why" questions that can wear a father out. They also increase their ability to focus for longer periods of time, especially on things they find interesting. They begin to understand that other people have different perspectives and feelings than they do. As more children enter preschool programs, they are introduced to numbers, shapes, colors, and letters. Some of the cognitive milestones include:

◆ 3-year-olds can do simple puzzles, name colors, and start doing pretend play.
◆ 4-year-olds begin to understand counting and time. They may start playing board games and remember stories. They will let you know if you have left out a page or even a word from a familiar story.

These are some of the typical skills that children learn at home and in preschool, where they are also introduced to letters and begin to think about and work with the sounds (phonemes) in words.

Children at this age make sense of the world by putting things into categories, such as animals, gender, vehicles, dinosaurs. Their increased capacity with language helps them organize their experiences. Their perception of the world still often involves fantasy and an interest and attraction to superheroes with magical powers. They may also have problems with perception and make judgements based on appearance, for example, thinking that a tall, skinny glass holds more water than a short, fat glass. The increase in children's vocabulary leads to greater ability to understand both the world and self.

One area of cognitive development in young children that has been studied in great depth has been early literacy. Language and literacy development have been highlighted over the past 20 years. Young children from ages 2–5 are learning language at an amazing rate, from 200 words to 10,000 words in their vocabularies. This is an area where fathers have the potential to make a significant impact on early learning and later school success.There are many ways for fathers to support literacy. They can model reading, read to the child, create opportunities for verbal interaction, and introduce new words.[46] Research indicates that 75% of fathers read to their children ages 0–4, on average from daily to three times per week.[47] Nichols articulates differences between fathers and mothers in reading to young children.[48] Mothers are more aware of the importance of early literacy and spend more time than fathers in reading. The benefits of reading to children include fostering emotional security, aiding relaxation (not only helping children fall asleep, but parents falling asleep while reading to children), and sharing values with children.[49] Children whose fathers read to them become better readers, perform better in school, and develop better relationship skills.[50]

Early literacy programs have helped support the important role that fathers play in introducing their children to the world of books and learning as a foundation for school success.[51] Researchers found that a 6-week Head Start program to support children's literacy development led fathers to be more committed to literacy development and increased their confidence and sense of agency.[52] Glen created a 6-week Dads and Kids book club to strengthen father–child relationships through shared literacy activities and give dads new ideas and strategies for supporting early literacy. The program used literacy-related activities including dramatic play, food preparation, and arts and crafts. The program focused on books about fathers as positive role models. Fathers were given a book to take home that allowed them to practice some of the reading skills that had been modeled by a male early childhood educator. Fathers reported that the program increased their understanding of children and literacy development, provided new ideas about reading, and increased their enjoyment of reading to their children.[53]

## Emotional Development

The preschool years are an important time in the development of emotional understanding and learning to regulate emotions. This is the beginning of the development of emotional intelligence. Preschoolers learn the names of different emotions and better understand emotions in themselves and in others. Early educators often talk about the big, sometimes overwhelming feelings that children have. John Gottman and colleagues have developed a program to help parents understand their thinking about emotions.[54] The program helps parents to reflect on how their own parents responded to their childhood expressions of emotions and how that has impacted their own ability to express a wide range of emotions. Glen has adopted Gottman's father-friendly language of emotion coaching with fathers.[55] There are four main parenting styles of approaching emotions:

- ◆ The *dismissive parent* does not want to dwell on negative emotions such as sadness or fear.
- ◆ The *disapproving parent* does not want to accept the child's feelings (e.g., fear or anger).
- ◆ The *permissive parent* has empathy for the child but does not help by giving limits to expression.
- ◆ The *emotion coaching parent* understands the child's emotions and is willing to walk through difficult emotions and help the child toward greater understanding and problem-solving.

These styles have some similarity to the different parenting styles discussed earlier in the chapter. Text Box 5.4 lists emotion coaching steps. A program for fathers that focused on emotion coaching strategies, called Dads Tuning into Kids, found positive results for both fathers and children.[56] Fathers reported increases in positive socialization of emotions in their children and a reduction in difficult behaviors. Fathers also experienced greater parenting satisfaction and efficacy.

---

**TEXT BOX 5.4**

**Steps for Emotion Coaching: Ways of "Being With" Your Child**

1. **Emotional awareness**—be aware of your child's emotions and your own emotions in response to the child's emotions.
2. **Connect with the child** during an emotional episode—empathize and stay with your child until they are calm and are able to think clearly. Take control as needed during this time.
3. **Listen to the child** to understand their perspective and think about the situation. Ask questions to clarify as needed.
4. **Name emotions**—Help your child to put names to feelings and help older children to identify mixed feelings.
5. **Set limits** and **teach acceptable expression** of emotions.
6. **Provide guidance** on how to regulate emotions.
7. **Find good solutions**—Work with your child to identify potential solutions and find one that works for both of you.

Source: Adapted from Gottman et al. (1996).

---

**Understanding Self**. Children begin to acquire a sense of self-understanding during the preschool years. This includes a beginning sense of *self-concept* and *self-esteem*. Self-concept refers to what one believes about oneself. Children's self-concept includes a wide range of beliefs about their physical characteristics, behaviors, and competencies. The preschool years are a critical time for developing a self-concept that includes *gender identity, racial identity*, and a *sense of self-esteem*.

*Gender identity* describes a person's psychological sense of their gender.[57] *Gender expression* is how one portrays their gender to others. This may include behavior, hairstyle, or clothing. By age 3, children most often identify themselves by the sex they were assigned at birth based on their genitalia. They try to make sense of gender by observing others in their world and external signs of gender expression. Children intuit the importance of gender in society. Exploration of gender for 3–5-year-olds is typical and most children by age 5 have developed a stable gender identity. For young children, this may be expressed by the toys they choose to play with or dressing up in different clothes during pretend play. They are influenced by gender stereotypes and may grow rigid in their ideas about girls and boys. Fathers play an important role through their own expression of gender.

We are learning that young children are more aware of race than researchers previously thought.[58] This is a more salient issue for children of color, especially Black children, who get social messages about not being as good as White children. It is a critical time for fathers to pay attention to the social perceptions that children are developing around race. Fathers of children of color have to work harder to create a social environment that promotes a positive self-image to counter negative stereotypes. This is also an opportunity to talk about social justice around race differences and read books that include characters from different groups and stories that describe racial bias as a starting point for discussion about social justice.

**Fathers and Self-Esteem**. Self-esteem is a concept that is defined in different ways and often confused with self-confidence, which can turn into arrogance. A healthy sense of self-esteem is a genuine understanding and respect for one's own abilities. Dorothy Briggs describes the importance of early childhood years for developing positive self-esteem.[59] The child develops a sense of self-respect and a feeling of self-worth that forms the core of their personality. Jean Clarke, in her writings on self-esteem as a family affair, identifies two basic components of self-esteem—being loveable and being capable.[60] Fathers play a significant role in a child's developing self-esteem through their parenting style, play, and in the quality of the interactions that they have with their child. Fathers' tendency to connect to the outside world[61] helps children look at themselves and start comparing their abilities to others, which leads to feelings about being capable and good.

Fathers influence self-esteem in children through both their words and actions. It is essential to focus on both the "loveable" and "capable" aspects of self-esteem. Showing genuine affection and spending time with young children demonstrates that they are loveable. As young children explore the world around them, fathers' respect for their thinking and effort helps them to feel capable. Self-esteem is compromised by insecure attachment, excessive parental expectations, harsh punishment, expressions of negative views of the child, and frequent rejection.[62] Having expectations that are too high can lead to a child feeling they are not capable. Praise that is too high can give a young child a false sense of competence. Young children look to their fathers for acceptance and support and thrive when they hear and receive them in concrete ways.

## Challenges for Fathers

Some important, large social-system realities challenge parents today. First, is the need for childcare for working parents and to the difficulties in finding high quality childcare and early education programs. The second is the proliferation of digital devices, including smart watches, smart phones, tablets, and computers, as well as television screens. How do these impact young children and how should fathers manage their own and children's time with these devices? Finally, some fathers may be challenged by having a child with special needs and by the need to access help for the child and family.

## Childcare and Family Support

Most families with preschool children must find early childhood care and education programs. According to the Council of Economic Advisors, out-of-home programs are used by 60% of families with preschoolers.[63] The two biggest challenges that families encounter are accessibility of care and cost of care. A significant number (27%) of families cannot find care and the cost of care varies depending upon where families live. In 2022 dollars, the cost of care for 3–5-year-olds in home-based programs ranged from US$6,000–US$10,000 per year; center-based programs cost from US$7,000–US$12,000 per year.[64] Families living in large urban areas pay more than families in smaller cities or rural areas. Low-income families may be eligible for Head Start or other state-sponsored preschool programs if spaces are available. Some states offer Universal Pre-K programs at no cost.

Families also look for the right fit for their child and may prefer certain types of early education.[65] Programs range from traditional nursery schools that focus on free play to more academic programs that focus on school readiness. It takes time and resources for families to find the best fit for their child. Fathers and mothers also have to consider what their needs are. A final step in selecting a program or caregiver is to visit a program and observe the relationship skills of the caregiver or teacher by considering the following questions:[66]

♦ How are teachers and children getting along?
♦ How do teachers talk with the children?
♦ How do teachers guide and redirect children?
♦ How do teachers communicate with fathers?

Jay and Glen have written that fathers can view early childhood programs as more than just dropping off their child.[67] Father involvement in early childhood programs can take many different forms[68] and early childhood programs would like to see more father involvement. This is an opportunity for fathers to partner with early childhood programs and staff to be involved in attending special programs, parent groups, and volunteering in the classroom. Fathers can better understand the program and observe their child in the classroom. Fathers of young children reported in a survey that it was very important to attend parent–teacher meetings, program events, and events geared for fathers, as well as doing drop off and pick up.[69] There are also opportunities for fathers to serve on advisory or other types of committees. Program staff appreciate bringing a male presence into classrooms that are often female-dominated. Fathers can benefit from this involvement by learning more about their child and having an influence on the program quality.

## Managing Screen Time

Fathers of young children are faced with the challenge of managing their child's interaction and amount of "screen time." Home computers, smart phones, and tablets have been added to the large-screen TVs that populate most homes. The general advice from the American Academy of Pediatrics and the World Health Organization has been to limit 3–5-year-olds to one hour of high-quality screen time per day. Recent research from Canada tracked parent reports of screen time compared to teacher reports on developmental health.[70] The researchers found that children with more than one hour of daily screen time were more likely to be vulnerable in five different domains: physical health, social competence, emotional maturity, language and cognitive development, and communication skills.[71] The concern about physical health and obesity has been around for a while and seems to have an obvious connection with passive screen time. This type of finding affirms the current guidelines for preschoolers.

These general guidelines seem reasonable on the surface, but the ubiquity of screens in homes raises further questions for researchers and the need for more nuanced advice for parents. Fathers and mothers who are constantly looking at their smart phones model a "screen time" behavior for young children, who are very curious about this device that takes so much of their parents' attention.

The new technologies can be beneficial for families. Glen, as a grandparent of preschoolers who live halfway across the country, finds FaceTime calls to be fun and helpful in maintaining a relationship at a distance. His grandchildren often sit while he reads books to them or will want him to tell them a story. There are also some high-quality children's TV programs that have positive impacts on early literacy and social–emotional development.[72] The American Academy of Pediatricians website, healthychildren.org, suggests useful guidelines for parents of preschoolers to think about in using media beyond limiting screen time (see Text Box 5.5).

---

**TEXT BOX 5.5**

**Guidelines for Media Use**

◆ Limit screen use to no more than one hour a day
◆ Find other activities that are healthy for bodies and minds
◆ Select media that is interactive, nonviolent, educational, and prosocial
◆ Watch together and interact with your child

Source: Healthychildren.org.

---

Fathers should be mindful of their own use of digital media and what this models for their children. Some questions to reflect on about personal screen use and parenting are as follows.

### Reflection Questions
◆ How often do you check your phone for email or text messages while you are with your children?
◆ What types of TV do your children observe that you watch?
◆ How do you select TV programs for your children that are consistent with your values?
◆ How can you help your young children to become careful consumers of media?
◆ What are interactive and creative ways to use digital media with young children?

Maryanne Wolf has taken a careful look at the reading brain in the digital world.[73] She recommends that parents consider the appropriateness of educational apps by thinking about the individual child, the content, and the context for using the app. Despite the prevalence of programs and apps, reading a book or telling stories at bedtime to preschool children is the most important thing that fathers can do to support their child's early literacy skills and pass on moral lessons.

## Understanding Special Needs in Early Childhood

One challenge in parenting young children is identifying if your child has special developmental or mental health needs. Of children ages 2–8, one in six has a developmental, mental health, or behavioral problem.[74] The process for identification is not always simple or clear. A health care provider may notice that there is a developmental delay and suggest further assessment. Preschool screening can also identify special needs. Preschool special education services are available for children who go through a thorough developmental assessment. If a child meets the criteria for special education services, then school districts are required to provide services. Young children may also be assessed for mental health and developmental concerns through the Diagnostic Classification of Mental Health and Developmental Disorders of Infancy and Early Childhood (DC-0-5) assessment process to identify mental health challenges that can be treated by mental health specialists.[75] The DC-0-5 is an age-appropriate way to assess infants, toddlers, and preschool children.

If your child has been identified with a special need, it is important to intervene early. Fathers may find it difficult to learn that their child has a special need or they may be relieved to find out about a concern that they were not sure about. Fathers are often concerned about children being stigmatized when they receive a diagnostic label. The role of fathers who want the best for their children is to advocate for the child to get their needs met and find the best fit for services.

Fathers of young children with special needs often report experiencing feelings of guilt, disappointment, lack of control, and isolation.[76] They often have lower levels of satisfaction with family life. Fathers who access social supports frequently report that having a child with special needs leads to personal growth. The coparent relationship may also be impacted and can be more stressful for fathers. Fathers also may worry about the financial costs of having a child with special needs; they may feel a need to work longer hours. This can lead to a cycle of being less involved with both the child and family and more isolated and less satisfied with family life. Fathers of young children with special needs need to be open to asking for help and support for the child and themselves. Fathers can be a protective factor for children with special needs and an important support for mothers.[77]

## Summary

An important theme of this chapter is that parenting style and positive parenting behaviors related to attachment are strongly associated with multiple areas of child development, including mental health, cognitive skills, social skills, and emotional development. Decades of research have shed light on positive parenting behaviors such as warmth, sensitivity, responsiveness, reasonable expectations, and firm limits as beneficial to children. Father–child play is an important vehicle for building positive relationships. Play has an impact on all aspects of development in early childhood. Fathers are an important connection to the outside world for young children and have a responsibility to help children explore and provide a safe haven in a changing world.

## Notes

1 Davies, D. (2011). *Child development: A practitioner's guide* (3rd ed.). Guilford Press.
2 Shipley, K. G., & McAfee, J. G. (2015). *Assessment in speech-language pathology: A resource manual* (5th ed.). Cengage Learning.
3 Zosh, J. M., Hassinger-Das, B., & Laurie, M. (2022). *Learning through play and the development of holistic skills across childhood.* The LEGO Foundation.
4 Ferreira, T., Cadima, J., Matias, M., Vieira, J. M., Leal, T., & Matos, P. M. (2016). Preschool children's prosocial behavior: The role of mother–child,

father–child and teacher–child relationships. *Journal of Child & Family Studies, 25*, 1829–1839. https://doi.org/10.1007/s10826-016-0369-x

5 Galinsky, E. (1987). *The six stages of parenthood.* Perseus Books.

6 Pleck, J. H. (1997). Paternal involvement: Levels, sources, and consequences. In M. E. Lamb (Ed.), *The role of the father in child development* (3rd ed., pp. 66–103). John Wiley & Sons.

7 Galinsky, E. (1987). *The six stages of parenthood.*

8 Kuppens, S., & Ceulemans, E. (2019). Parenting styles: A closer look at a well-known concept. *Journal of Child and Family Studies, 28*, 168–181. https://doi.org/10.1007/s10826-018-1242-x

9 Baumrind, D. (1971). Current patterns of parental authority. *Developmental Psychology, 4*, 1–103. https://doi.org/10.1037/h0030372

10 Bibi, F., Chaudhry, A. G., Awan, E. A., & Tariq, B. (2013). Contributions of parenting styles in the life domain of children. *Journal of Humanities and Social Sciences, 12*(2),91–95. https://doi.org/10.9790/0837-1229195

11 Kuppens, S., & Ceulemans, E. (2019). Parenting styles.

12 Williams, L. R., Degnan, K. A., Perez-Edgar, K. E., Henderson, H. A., Rubin, K. H., Pine, D. S., Steinberg, L., & Fox, N. A. (2009). Impact of behavioral inhibition and parenting style on internalizing and externalizing problems from early childhood through adolescence. *Journal of Abnormal Child Psychology, 37*(8), 1063–1075. https://doi.org/10.1007/s10802-009-9331-3

13 Mehus, C. J., & Patrick, M. E. (2021). Prevalence of spanking in US national samples of 35-year-old parents from 1993–2017. *JAMA Pediatrics, 175*(1), 92–94. https://doi.org/10.1001/jamapediatrics.2020.2197

14 Yaffe, Y. (2020). Systematic review of the differences between mothers and fathers in parenting styles and practices. *Current Psychology, 42*, 16011–16024. https://doi.org/10.1007/s12144-020-01014-6

15 University of Minnesota Extension. (1997). *Positive parenting curriculum.* Author.

16 Yaffe, Y. (2020). Systematic review of the differences between mothers and fathers.

17 Tavassolie, T., Dudding, S., Madigan, A. L., Thorvardarson, E., & Winsler, A. (2016). Differences in perceived parenting style between mothers and fathers: Implications for child outcomes and marital conflict. *Journal of Child and Family Studies, 25*, 2055–2068. https://doi.org/10.1007/s10826-016-0376-y

18 Palm, G. (1992). Building intimacy and parenting skills through father–child activity time. In L. Johnson & G. Palm (Eds.), *Working with fathers: Methods and perspectives* (pp. 79–100). Nu Ink.

19 Hirsh-Pasek, K., & Hadani, H. S. (2020). A new path to education reform: Playful learning promotes 21st-century skills in schools and beyond. Brookings Institute. https://www.brookings.edu/wp-content/uploads/2020/10/Big-Ideas_Hirsh-Pasek_PlayfulLearning.pdf

20 Zosh, J. M., Hassinger-Das, B., & Laurie, M. (2022). Learning through play.

21 Amodia-Bidakowska, A., Laverty, C., & Ramchandani, P. G. (2020). Father–child play: A systematic review of its frequency, characteristics and potential impact on children's development. *Developmental Review, 57*, 100924. https://doi.org/10.1016/j.dr.2020.100924

22 Cabrera, N., & Roggman, L. (2017). Father play: Is it special? *Infant Mental Health Journal, 38*, 706–708, p. 708. https://doi.org/10.1002/imhj.21680

23 Robinson, E. L., St. George, J., & Freeman, E. E. (2021). A systematic review of father–child play interactions and the impacts on child development. *Children, 8*,389. https://doi.org/10.3390/children8050389

24 Meuwissen, A. S., & Carlson, S. M. (2015). Fathers matter: The role of father parenting in preschoolers' executive function development. *Journal of Experimental Child Psychology, 140*, 1–15. https://doi.org/10.1016/j.jecp.2015.06.010

25 Gauvain, M. (2018). Cognitive development. In M. H. Borenstein (Ed.), *The Sage encyclopedia of lifespan human development.* https://doi.org/10.4135/9781506307633

26 Robinson, E. L., St. George, J., & Freeman, E. E. (2021). A systematic review of father–child play.

27 Zosh, J. M., Hassinger-Das, B., & Laurie, M. (2022). Learning through play.

28 Robinson, E. L., St. George, J., & Freeman, E. E. (2021). A systematic review of father–child play.

29 Meuwissen, A. S., & Carlson, S. M. (2015). Fathers matter.

30 Zosh, J. M., Hassinger-Das, B., & Laurie, M. (2022). Learning through play.

31 Zosh, J. M., Hassinger-Das, B., & Laurie, M. (2022). Learning through play; Robinson, E. L., St. George, J., & Freeman, E. E. (2021). A systematic review of father–child play.

32 Meuwissen, A. S., & Carlson, S. M. (2015). Fathers matter.

33 Davies, D. (2011). *Child development: A practitioner's guide.*

34 Paris, J., Ricardo, A., & Rymond, D. (2019). *Child growth and development.* College of the Canyons. https://open.umn.edu/opentextbooks/textbooks/750

35 Vollmer, R. L., Adamsons, K., Foster, J. S., & Mobley, A. R. (2015). Association of fathers' feeding practices and feeding style on preschool age children's diet quality, eating behavior and body mass index. *Appetite, 89*, 274–281. https://doi.org/10.1016/j.appet.2015.02.021

36 Morgan, P. J., Grounds, J. A., Ashton, L. M., Collins, C. E., Barnes, A. T., Pollock, E. R., Kennedy, S.-L., Rayward, A. T., Saunders, K. L., Drew, R. J., & Young, M. D. (2022). Impact of the "Healthy Youngsters, Healthy Dads" program on physical activity and other health behaviors: A randomized controlled trial involving fathers and their preschool-aged children. *BMC Public Health, 22*, 1166.https://doi.org/10.1186/s12889-022-13424-1

37 Dewar, G. (2020). Infant toilet training: The scientific evidence. https://parentingscience.com/infant-toilet-training/

38 Geasler, M. J., Dannison, L. I., & Edlund, C. J. (1995). Sexuality education of young children: Parental concerns. *Family Relations, 44*, 184–188.

39 American Academy of Pediatrics Council on Child Abuse and Neglect. (2023). Sexual behaviors in young children: What's normal, what's not. https://www.healthychildren.org/English/ages-stages/preschool/Pages/Sexual-Behaviors-Young-Children.aspx

40 Chrisman, K., & Couchenour, D. (2002). *Healthy sexuality development: A guide for early childhood educators and families.* National Association for the Education of Young Children.

41 American Academy of Pediatrics Council on Child Abuse and Neglect. (2023). Sexual behaviors in young children.

42 Wong, T. K. Y., Konishi, C., & Kong, X. (2020). Parenting and prosocial behavior: A meta-analysis. *Review of Social Development, 30*(2). https://doi.org/10.1111/sode.12481

43 Ferreira, T., Cadima, J., Matias, M., Vieira, J. M., Leal, T., & Matos, P. M. (2016). Preschool children's prosocial behavior.

44 Palm, G. (2007). The developmental journey: Fathers and children learning together. In S. E. Brotherson & J. M. White (Eds.), *Why fathers count* (pp. 163–176). Men's Studies Press.

45 Davies, D. (2011). *Child development: A practitioner's guide.*
46 Hess, R., & Holloway, S. (1984). Family and school educational institutions. In R. D. Parke (Ed.), *Review of child development research, 7: The family* (pp. 179–222). University of Chicago Press.
47 Palm, G. (2013). Fathers and early literacy. In J. Pattnaik (Ed.), *Father involvement in young children's lives* (pp. 13–30). Springer.
48 Nichols, S. (2000). Unsettling the bedtime story: Parents' reports of home literacy practices. *Contemporary Issues in Early Childhood, 1*(3), 315–328. https://doi.org/10.2304/ciec.2000.1.3.7
49 Flouri, E. (2005). *Fathering and child outcomes.* John Wiley and Sons; Ortiz, R. (2000). The many faces of learning to read: The role of fathers in helping their children to develop early literacy skills. *Multicultural Perspectives, 2*(2), 10–17.
50 Green, S. (2002). Involving fathers in children's literacy development: An introduction to the Fathers Reading Every Day (FRED) program. *Journal of Extension, 40*(5). https://tigerprints.clemson.edu/joe/vol40/iss5/18/
51 Chacko, A., Fabiano, G. A., Doctoroff, G. L., & Fortson, B. (2018). Engaging fathers in effective parenting for preschool children using shared book reading: A randomized controlled trial. *Journal of Clinical Child Adolescent Psychology, 47*(1), 79–93. https://doi.org/10.1080/15374416.2016.1266648
52 Bauman, D. C., & Wasserman, K. B. (2010). Empowering fathers of disadvantaged preschoolers to take a more active role in preparing their children for literacy success at school. *Early Childhood Education Journal, 37,* 363–370. https://doi.org/10.1007/s10643-009-0367-3
53 Palm, G. (2013). Fathers and early literacy.
54 Gottman, J. M., Fainsilber-Katz, L., & Hoven, C. (1996). Parental meta-emotion philosophy and the emotional life of families: Theoretical models and preliminary data. *Journal of Family Psychology, 10,*243–268. https://doi.org/10.1037/0893-3200.10.3.243
55 Gottman, J. (with DeClaire, J.) (1997). *The heart of parenting: How to raise an emotionally intelligent child.* Simon and Schuster.
56 Havighurst, S. S., Wilson, K. R., Harley, A. E., & Kehoe, C. E. (2019). Dads tuning in to kids: A randomized controlled trial of an emotion socialization parenting program for fathers. *Social Development, 28*(4), 979–997. https://doi.org/10.1111/sode.12375
57 American Psychological Association. (2015). *Gender.* https://apastyle.apa.org/style-grammar-guidelines/bias-free-language/gender
58 Davies, D. (2011). *Child development: A practitioner's guide.*
59 Briggs, D. (1988). *Your child's self-esteem.* Broadway Books.
60 Clarke, J. I. (1998). *Self-esteem: A family affair.* Hazelden.
61 Paquette, D., & St. George, J. (2023). Proximate and ultimate mechanisms of human father–child rough-and-tumble play. *Neuroscience an Biobehavioral Reviews,* 105151. https://doi.org/10.1016/j.neubiorev.2023.105151
62 Davies, D. (2011). *Child development: A practitioner's guide.*
63 Council of Economic Advisors. (2023). Improving access, affordability, and quality in early care and education (ECE) market. https://www.whitehouse.gov/cea/written-materials/2023/07/18/improving-access-affordability-and-quality-in-the-early-care-and-education-ece-market/
64 Landivar, L. C., Graf, N. L., & Rayo, G. A. (2023, January). *Childcare prices in local areas: Initial findings from the National Database of Childcare Prices.* Women's Bureau Issue Brief. U.S. Department of Labor. https://www.dol.gov/sites/dolgov/files/WB/NDCP/WB_IssueBrief-NDCP-final.pdf

65 Paris, J., Ricardo, A., & Rymond, D. (2019). *Child growth and development.*

66 Lepore, J. (2017). 5 must ask questions for parents in search of the best early childhood program. https://psychlearningcurve.org/questions-about -early-childhood-programs/

67 Fagan, J., & Palm, G. (2004). *Fathers and early childhood programs.* Cengage.

68 Fitzpatrick, T. (2011). *Linking fathers: Father involvement in early childhood programs.* Minnesota Fathers and Families Network.

69 Fitzpatrick, T. (2011). *Linking fathers: Father involvement in early childhood programs.*

70 Kerai, S., Almas, A., Guhn, M., Forer, B., & Oberle, E.(2022). Screen time and developmental health: Results from an early childhood study in Canada. *BMC Public Health, 22,* 310. https://doi.org/10.1186/s12889-022-12701-3

71 Muppalla, S., Vuppalapati, S., Reddy Pulliahgaru, A., & Sreenivasulu, H. (2023). Effects of excessive screen time on child development: An updated review and strategies for management. *Cureus, 15*(6), e40608. https://doi.org /10.7759/cureus.40608

72 Pappas, S. (2022). What do we really know about kids and screens? *Monitor on Psychology, 51*(3), 42. https://www.apa.org/monitor/2020/04/cover-kids -screens

73 Wolf, M. (2019). *Reader come home: The reading brain in a digital world.* HarperCollins.

74 Robinson, L. R., Holbrook, J. R., Bitsko, R. H., Hartwig, S. A., Kaminski, J. W., Ghandour, R. M., Peacock, G., Heggs, A., & Boyle, C. A. (2017). Differences in health care, family, and community factors associated with mental, behavioral, and developmental disorders among children aged 2–8 years in rural and urban areas—United States, 2011–2012. *Morbidity and Mortality Weekly Report, Surveillance Summaried, 66*(8), 1–11. http://dx.doi.org/10.15585 /mmwr.ss6608a1

75 Zero to Three. (2021). *DC:0-5™: Diagnostic classification of mental health and developmental disorders of infancy and early childhood* (Version 2.0). www.zero-tothree.org/our-work/learn-professional-development/dc0-5-manual-and -training/

76 National Responsible Fatherhood Clearinghouse. (n.d.). *Supporting fathers of children with special needs.* https://www.fatherhood.gov/sites/default/files/ resource_files/e000004142.pdf

77 Fathers.com. (n.d.). *6 thoughts for dads of children with special needs.* https:// fathers.com/blog/your-situation/special-needs-kids/6-thoughts-for-dads -of-special-needs-children/

# Fathers and Middle Childhood

Entry into School and Learning about the World

*I love the conversations that we have going between activities like a 45-minute conversation about [his new role as a hockey referee] … after his practice. Conversations about a movie that we watched together. Sometimes I feel like a pushover or I get really strict. It is hard to be in the middle and finding a good balance of my reactions. I have learned that I don't have to be so strict or rigid, I can be more flexible. I can give them more space to develop their own personalities. I am learning to trust them to be responsible.*

—Father of two sons, ages 9 and 13

## Introduction

Middle childhood is the stage of development between ages 6 and 12. Children gain the basic tools, skills, and motivations to become happy and productive members of society during these years. They start formal education between ages 5 and 7, learn to read and do basic math, interact with peers and adults outside the family, take responsibility and develop self-control, and engage in group activities. Children must learn to sit still, follow directions, and perform autonomously to benefit from school. The early school years are essential to later development. Aletha Huston and Marika Ripke have written that third grade achievement in school is a strong predictor of academic performance in high school and post-secondary school. By ages 10 to 12, children enter middle school, reach puberty, and experience a growth spurt.[1] This chapter addresses both the developmental tasks of

DOI: 10.4324/9781003486107-6

fathers and fathers' contributions to the healthy development of their school-age children.

## Developmental Tasks of Fathers during Middle Childhood

Many changes occur during middle childhood that affect fathers. Children become more independent, are better able to care for themselves, and assume more responsibility for themselves. These changes are clearly articulated in the quotation at the beginning of this chapter. A major theme during this period is that fathers support children's independence and help children assume more responsibility for themselves. Fathers support children by assigning simple household chores, helping them organize and be responsible for their school backpack, communicating with them about school, and much more. The changes that occur during middle childhood mean that fathers and mothers do not need to spend as much time with children as they did during earlier years. Fathers may have more time to enjoy activities that they put aside when children were younger. Engaging in activities that were put aside allows fathers to grow and develop as adults. Many children begin to have sleepovers at friends' or relatives' homes during middle childhood. These breaks from children give fathers more time to spend with the child's mother or other adults in ways that are rewarding and support adult relationship growth.

As children grow older, fathers may become more established in their careers and take on greater responsibility at work. These changes are not so much the result of children's aging but are related to fathers' maturity and experience. Career advancement and added work-related responsibilities can mean that fathers' income increases. Mothers may also experience financial benefits from their own career advancement. These financial gains can provide greater family stability and a sense of well-being for all family members.

### Work–Family Balance

Added workplace responsibilities can also lead to greater challenges with balancing work and family. A 2018 study conducted by the Pew Research Center found that 63% of fathers felt they spent too little time with their children.[2] Fathers may find that the demands of work create stress that spills over to the home environment, called work–family stress. Work–family balance has been defined as the "extent to which an individual is equally engaged in and equally satisfied with his or her work role and family role."[3] Work–family stress and inability to balance work and family demands can have a negative impact on fathers' emotional and physical availability to children. Employed mothers may also experience work–family stress. In Chapter 1, we described how people's lives are embedded in multiple systems that sometimes affect each other (called the ecological-systems perspective). For example, mothers' workplace stress may have a negative impact on fathers' sense of work–family balance and vice versa. The interactions of these systems are called cross-over effects. Jay and his colleagues found that mothers reported lower levels of work–family balance when fathers were less engaged with children under age 13 and when fathers had less flexible work schedules.[4]

There are many fathers who face significant workplace challenges. They may change jobs frequently, become unemployed, or have jobs that become obsolete. These stresses can also spill over into fathers' parenting.[5] These fathers may become less emotionally available to children, react negatively when children misbehave, or withdraw from parenting. Fathers and mothers can reflect on their family and work situations and try to find an arrangement that limits stress and promotes well-being. Fathers may want to reflect on the following questions regarding work and money.

### Reflection Questions

◆ Do you constantly think about work when you are home at the expense of being involved with your children?

◆ Do you easily become angry and upset with your children because of workplace stress?

◆ Are you frequently worrying about money and not enjoying your time with children?

◆ Are you and your child's mother arguing about work or money in front of the children?

## Developing Shared Interests

Fathers' growth and development may also occur as a result of shared interests with children that draw fathers and children closer together. Children may become interested in their father's hobbies or activities, or fathers may become interested in their children's hobbies or activities. Shared activities are more enjoyable during middle childhood because children's average attention span increases from about 10 minutes for 4-year-olds to almost 20–30 minutes for school-age children. For example, shared activities such as fishing or cooking are now more feasible because of children's improved attention span. These shared interests have the potential to strengthen the bond between father and child, which in turn may positively affect fathers' well-being.

## Understanding Family Significance

Despite children's growing independence, families are still at the center of children's lives during middle childhood. The architect of the ecological-systems perspective, Urie Bronfenbrenner, acknowledged that family is the main "engine of development."[6] Fathers and mothers are essential to children's achievements and well-being. Parents create the structures that guide children's lives and provide them with the skills for everyday living. They make sure that children are ready for school in the morning, get sufficient sleep, dress appropriately, visit the doctor, and obtain school supplies. They prepare their meals and ensure that children eat nutritious foods. They provide opportunities for children to play with peers, participate in sports or arts activities, obtain religious education, have access to books, and experience enriching activities outside of the home. They provide guidance to children and model the values that are important to them. The list of what parents do for their children is endless.

According to the ecological-systems perspective, neighborhoods and communities also influence children's development. Fathers and mothers often give children more freedom to play outdoors with other children during middle childhood. While these environments affect children, one cannot ignore the role that parents play in deciding which environments children are exposed to. Parents select the neighborhoods where children live, the schools that they attend, and the doctors that they see. Parents assume a management role that affects every aspect of children's lives. That is not to say that parents have no constraints on the choices they make for their children. Poverty, lack of affordable housing, food insecurity, neighborhood crime, and lack of health care are significant constraints that affect all the choices that parents can make. These stresses often place considerable strain on father–child relationships. Programs that help fathers to meet basic needs can reduce parenting stress. One such program is the Affordable Care Act (see healthcare.gov) that provides health insurance at little to no cost.

## Coparenting

An important developmental parenting task during middle childhood is for fathers and mothers to maintain a healthy coparenting relationship. We have emphasized throughout this book the changes that occur as children grow and develop, but fathers and mothers also change. Father–mother coparenting relationships change as well. James McHale and his colleagues have suggested that coparenting relationships undergo some reorganization as children mature or as new children are born.[7] For example, mothers who stayed home with children or worked part-time during the early childhood years may decide to go back to work full-time. Fathers and mothers may need to renegotiate how they share parenting roles to accommodate the mother's work schedule and the needs of children. Reorganization of coparenting roles can require significant adaptation on the part of fathers, mothers, and children. Fathers may need to assist more with getting children ready for school in the morning, or they may need to adjust their work schedules so that they can be available on some days after school.

In Chapter 1, we stated that there are both positive and negative components of coparenting relationships. Fathers and mothers frequently establish patterns of coparenting behavior when children are young. These are behaviors that fathers and mothers consistently repeat. Fathers and mothers who are supportive of each other as coparents when children are young are likely to be supportive of each other during middle childhood. Parents who engage in high levels of coparenting conflict early may do so in later years. This is not to say that parents cannot change. Change is always possible, but it requires parents to learn new patterns of relating to each other.

Fathers and mothers typically experience times when they are supportive of each other as coparents and other times when they have conflict. Conflict is common in father–mother relationships and only becomes a problem when it occurs far more than support or when it is intense and frequent. In Chapter 5, we stated that coparenting disagreements and conflict can arise when fathers and mothers differ in their parenting styles (such as expectations for child obedience). These differences can persist during middle childhood. Conflict between fathers and mothers can also arise over children's chores, homework, use of cell phones, and many other issues. Conflict often stems from differences in values and beliefs about how to parent. For example, fathers may feel that children should be punished for "talking back" to their parents, whereas mothers may feel that children should be given more leeway to express anger or question what a parent is saying. These differences are frequently rooted in the way parents were raised. It can be helpful for fathers and mothers to examine the underlying reasons for their differences. Also, fathers and mothers can learn to compromise and respect each other's parenting style. Here are some helpful self-reflection questions.

## Reflection Questions

- ◆ Do you criticize or blame the mother of your child for your child's misbehavior?
- ◆ Do you listen to your child's mother when she is speaking about your child or about your parenting differences?
- ◆ When you and your partner do not agree on an issue, do you try to work out a compromise?
- ◆ What are your children learning from watching you interact with their mother?
- ◆ How can you model respect for the mother of your child so that your child will also show respect for her?

# Understanding School-Age Child Development

The important developmental tasks of middle childhood generally fall into four broad areas: establishing a healthy lifestyle (e.g., learning to eat healthy foods), learning a wide range of skills (e.g., reading, writing, numeracy), learning to assume responsibility and control over one's emotions and behavior, and navigating the social world of peers. Fathers contribute in important ways to each of these areas of development. Studies have shown that fathers contribute to children's academic skills, peer relationships, and social–emotional development above and beyond the influences of mothers on children.[8] Decades of research have demonstrated the effects of mothers on children, but these studies did not include fathers.[9] In the early days of research studying fathers' influences on children, mothers were not included. An important development in recent years has been to include both fathers and mothers in research studies.[10] These studies are a vast improvement because they more accurately represent the reality of families. Children are affected by the important people in their lives. Fathers have a profound influence on children even though they may spend less time with children than mothers. Fathers who do not live in the same household with children also have a significant influence on them.[11]

## Physical Development

Children undergo tremendous physical growth during middle childhood. They typically gain five to seven pounds per year and grow about two inches per year.[12] They become more muscular and coordinated. As a result, they show improvement in their ability to engage in sports, ride a bicycle, swim, dance, and run. Fine motor skills also improve, allowing children to become more adept at writing, cutting, drawing, and painting.

**Promoting Healthy Eating.** Eating nutritional foods helps children to grow and develop into healthy adolescents and adults. Children grow at a slower rate during middle childhood compared with early childhood, and it is important for parents to limit the amount of fat and processed food that children eat.

Children are at risk for obesity if they eat too much fat and sugar and engage in too little physical activity. Fathers have an important influence on children's eating behaviors, as they are role models of healthy eating and provide opportunities for children to engage in physical activity.

Contemporary fathers have greater influence on children's eating practices and food intake than fathers in past decades because men are more involved in meal preparation.[13] Fathers influence children's eating not only through the foods that they themselves like to eat, but also through their use of control of children's eating behavior. Fathers who place a lot of restrictions on foods tend to make those foods more desirable, while fathers who pressure children to eat certain foods make those foods less desirable. When fathers are highly restrictive and controlling of children's food choices, children are more likely to avoid foods such as fruits and vegetables, overeat or undereat, and desire to drink instead of eat.[14] In contrast, children are more likely to eat fruits and vegetables when fathers provide positive encouragement of healthy eating and make healthy foods available to children.[15]

The eating behaviors of many men differ in significant ways from those of women. Compared to women, men prefer more fatty foods with strong tastes, they eat more sweet or salty foods while watching television, and they eat more foods from fast food restaurants, which tend to have high fat, sugar, and salt content. This does not mean that all men eat more unhealthy foods than women. Many men make healthy food choices and many women make unhealthy food choices. Children learn to like and eat the foods that their parents expose them to.[16] They prefer to eat fatty and sweet foods when their fathers eat those same foods on a regular basis.

Fathers can promote healthy eating behaviors by modeling— purposefully demonstrating healthy food choices and eating behaviors (e.g., not eating snacks to excess between meals, eating balanced meals) intending to encourage children to do the same.[17] Fathers often feel a responsibility to model healthy eating and food choices for their children, but they also indicate there is a lack of accessible information about how to do that.[18] The

Loughborough University Child Feeding Guide provides excellent tips for modeling healthy eating (see Text Box 6.1).[19]

---

**TEXT BOX 6.1**

**Modeling Healthy Eating**

1. Eat together—plan to have family meals on the same days every week
2. Talk about healthy foods you enjoy
3. Avoid making negative comments about food
4. Use others as good role models—watching adults eat healthy foods influences children's choice of food

Source: Loughborough University Child Feeding Guide (2017).

---

**Promoting Physical Activity.** Children's physical activity plays an important role in their physical, emotional, and social health during middle childhood and in later years. Children who are more physically active are less likely to become obese, experience higher levels of self-esteem and well-being, and are more likely to be accepted by their peers.[20] School-age children can be physically active by playing outdoors with peers and parents, going to the playground or swimming pool, participating in organized sports, taking dance classes, and having access to physical education programs in schools.

Many children participate in organized sports in the United States and other countries. Organized sports take place in schools, communities (e.g., soccer leagues), religious organizations, and camp programs. Fathers may coach their children's sports activities or encourage children's participation by attending matches or practicing with children at home. Jay Coakley has suggested that fathers are more likely than mothers to monitor children's sports activities because they have more expertise (or claim to have more expertise) in sports.[21]

Sports are also an arena where gender attitudes and behaviors play out. In Chapter 1, we wrote that some men adhere to traditional values about masculinity while other men adhere to a "hybrid" view of masculinity that emphasizes nurturance and expressing feelings but also allows some traditional gender systems to remain intact. Coakley suggests that sports provide a context in which many men can engage with their children without challenging traditional gender ideologies. Fathers with traditional values about masculinity may view sports as a place where boys can be "made into men" in preparation for succeeding in a "man's world."[22] This does not mean that participation in sports should be limited to boys or that all traditional gendered behavior is healthy or appropriate. Fathers who teach their children to be aggressive in sports at all costs may make children anxious about losing and take the fun out of playing.

Some fathers have more progressive ideas about children's involvement in sports. These fathers may choose sports activities that emphasize gender equity, cooperation, and the pleasure of movement. For example, many communities in the United States offer co-ed sports such as softball or soccer for school-age children. Some children are very talented athletically. Their coaches may encourage fathers to enroll children in highly competitive teams, a decision that fathers and mothers can make together. Fathers may prefer that their children participate in equity-based sports but not want to hold their children back from reaching their full potential. A lot depends on what the child wants to do—as we have suggested in our discussion of the ecological-systems perspective, children play an important part in how fathers engage with them.

Just how much influence do fathers have over their children's engagement in physical activity? In a recent review of 20 physical activity studies that included both fathers and mothers, researchers found that parents of both sexes have about equivalent influence on their children's physical activity.[23] This review also found that fathers tend to have a greater influence on sons' physical activity whereas mothers tend to have a greater influence on daughters' physical activity.[24] These studies suggest that parents tend to model physical activity for same-sex children. Boys may like to throw a ball with their fathers. Girls may like to jump rope with their mothers. These preferences do not mean that all boys like to play catch or aren't interested in jumping rope, or that all girls like to jump rope or aren't interested in playing catch. Although there is some evidence that fathers influence physical activity more for sons, we cannot underestimate fathers' role as models of physical activity for both sons and daughters.[25] School-age children of both sexes are more likely to engage in physical activity when their fathers are physically active.[26]

## Emotional Development

Learning to assume responsibility for and control one's emotions and behavior is an important developmental task during middle childhood. In Chapter 3, we defined emotional development as the increasing capacity to experience, express, and interpret the full range of emotions and to cope with them appropriately. In early childhood, children experience a full range of emotions, including complex emotions such as jealousy and envy. However, they do not yet possess the vocabulary to label these emotions. Children's understanding and ability to express emotions expands dramatically in middle childhood. They can now express feelings such as anger or frustration without always having a temper tantrum or crying. They may still cry when upset, but they are also more likely to talk with their parents about their feelings. They can understand mixed emotions and may experience ambivalence. They also become better at hiding their emotions.

Children become increasingly competent at regulating their emotions. This includes the ability to monitor, evaluate, and modify emotional reactions (also called emotion regulation).[27] Children who can regulate their emotions can change the intensity of their emotional reactions to peers, family, and adults. Developmental psychologists generally agree that parents socialize children's emotion regulation by:

- ◆ Modeling emotion regulation for children (children observe their parents regulating their emotions during social interactions)
- ◆ Coaching children in effective strategies to regulate their emotions
- ◆ Providing a healthy family emotional climate

When fathers create a healthy emotional climate by reacting to their children's emotions with warmth, positivity, support, and sensitivity, children are better able to regulate their emotions.[28] In contrast, children have more difficulty with emotion regulation when fathers are harsh (through negative words or harsh discipline).[29] Children are also more likely to successfully regulate their emotions when fathers (and mothers) coach children by teaching them to problem solve when they are emotionally upset.[30] Essential steps for effective emotion coaching were presented in Chapter 5.

Emotional development is closely tied to social development in children because emotions take place mostly within the context of social relationships. The term *social–emotional development* is often used to describe the acquisition of skills for expressing emotions, regulating emotions, and managing social relationships within the family, school, and peer group.[31] Social–emotional development also includes the growth of children's self-understanding. Children in middle childhood have a more realistic sense of themselves than they do in early childhood. Their increased cognitive abilities enable them to think about their strengths and weaknesses rather than have an exaggerated sense of self. We wrote in Chapter 5 that self-understanding includes *self-concept* and *self-esteem*. Some children experience challenges with self-concept and self-esteem. Children who are repeatedly told by teachers and parents that they are not performing well in school or their behavior is problematic may develop a poor self-concept and low self-esteem. Children who have very low self-esteem may develop *learned helplessness*, the perception of complete lack of control in mastering tasks.[32]Learned helplessness is very similar to depression and may lead to significant mental health problems if it persists.

Fathers play a pivotal role in the development of children's self-concept and self-esteem. Children who think of their fathers and mothers as sources of support and comfort are likely to develop feelings of high self-esteem, positive thoughts about themselves (e.g., "I am smart"), and high emotion regulation.[33] Researchers have closely examined which aspects of fathers' parenting contribute to higher levels of self-esteem. In a study of 22 fourth- through seventh-grade classrooms, children reported higher levels of self-esteem when fathers praised them, engaged in positive communication, and were more affectionate.[34] In contrast, fathers' hostility toward children is a strong predictor of lower self-esteem. Parental hostility refers to rejection, neglect, maltreatment, punishment, and verbal and physical aggression. A systematic review of 35 studies from 16 countries found that children were significantly more likely to report lower self-esteem when both fathers and mothers engaged in hostile parenting.[35] Interestingly, the association between parental hostility and self-esteem was stronger for fathers than mothers.

The quality of father–child attachment is also crucial to children's healthy self-esteem. Recall that attachment refers to specific, enduring emotional bonds between people. Children who have insecure attachments with their fathers report significantly lower self-esteem during middle childhood than children with secure attachments to fathers.[36]

In summary, fathers play an important role in the development of children's emotional abilities during middle childhood, including their emotional expressions, emotion regulation, self-understanding, self-concept, and self-esteem. Text Box 6.2 suggests additional ways that fathers can help children become emotionally competent and have positive self-esteem.[37]

---

**TEXT BOX 6.2**

**Helping Children Become Emotionally Competent and Have Positive Self-Esteem**

- ◆ Model emotion regulation
- ◆ Create a healthy family climate in which everyone talks about emotions
- ◆ Help children cope with strong emotions
- ◆ Praise children when they label and express their feelings in appropriate ways
- ◆ Engage in positive communication
- ◆ Maintain an atmosphere low in hostility

Source: Weir (2023).

## Cognitive Development

School becomes a major part of children's lives during middle childhood. The start of schooling coincides with the development of more advanced cognitive abilities. These higher-level cognitive skills occur as a result of brain development and experience. Children can think more logically; understand concepts such as past, present, and future; and process more complex ideas such as addition, subtraction, and multiplication.[38] The development of children's executive functioning enables them to learn many new skills. Recall that executive functioning refers to the conscious control of thought and action, goal-directed responses, and self-regulatory ability.[39] Children's ability to pay attention and use memory strategies (an executive function) are important for learning. Memory strategies such as rehearsing and organizing new information make it more likely they will remember. Children may rehearse new information, such as their phone number, by repeating it until it is memorized. Organizing involves grouping information into categories by theme or type, such as animals or foods. These memory strategies enable children to acquire vast knowledge bases.

Fathers play an important role in helping children acquire cognitive skills. They can teach memory strategies, such as rehearsing new information until it is learned. They can help children make connections among new concepts, such as teaching that addition is the opposite of subtraction. Fathers can teach math by working on a household repair project with the child and teaching them to use a measuring tape, or can teach math and science while making muffins with the child letting them measure ingredients and talking about how the different ingredients change during baking.

The changing role of fathers has meant that many fathers are more engaged in children's education. In Chapter 1, we saw that mothers spent about triple the amount of time in educational activities with children under age 6. In middle childhood, the overall time spent in educational activities with children is just slightly higher for mothers than fathers (0.14 hours compared to 0.09 hours per day). An extensive review of 31 studies of fathers' and mothers' involvement in children's education concluded that despite the widespread belief that mothers are more central to children's education, both parents are about equally involved in their school-age children's education.[40] Interest in fathers' roles in child learning and education has grown during the past several decades, focused on fathers' help with homework, involvement in children's schools, attending school events, and reading to children.

**Helping Children with Homework.** Father engagement in children's education typically involves helping with homework and checking to make sure homework is completed. Children perform better in school when both fathers and mothers provide homework support.[41] Moreover, the influence that fathers and mothers have on child achievement is about equal.[42] Fathers' help with homework is not only beneficial to children's school achievement, but also is an opportunity for father–child relationships to grow and develop. Children are likely to feel supported by their fathers when they are engaged with homework. Helping with homework is an opportunity for fathers to become aware of their children's academic strengths and approaches to learning. Children may also talk about their experiences with teachers and peers during homework help that they would not otherwise share.

Nonetheless, the interactions that take place around homework may not always be positive. Conflict between fathers and children may occur when children have difficulty completing tasks or paying attention. Fathers may feel impatient with children who struggle with homework. The U.S. Department of Education provides helpful ideas about how to help children with homework. Text Box 6.3 is a partial list of tips for parents.

---

**TEXT BOX 6.3**

**Helping Your Child with Homework**

- ◆ Set a regular time for homework
- ◆ Pick a place
- ◆ Remove distractions
- ◆ Provide supplies and identify resources
- ◆ Set a good example
- ◆ Be interested and interesting

Source: U.S. Department of Education,
www2.ed.gov/parents/academic/help/homework/index.html.

**School Involvement.** Parent participation in children's schools (e.g., attending school functions, volunteering in the classroom) has received more attention in the United States since the federal government passed the No Child Left Behind Act in 2001, which stated that parent involvement is a condition of federal funding for schools. Since this legislation was passed, several programs have been implemented to involve fathers in children's schools. Strong Fathers Strong Families is one such program that is implemented throughout the United States and internationally.[43] This program provides training to school staff to learn how to better reach fathers in schools, conducts Bring Your Dads to School Day across schools throughout the country, and provides resources for fathers to engage children in learning activities at home. Strong Fathers Strong Families reports that it has involved more than 225,000 fathers in its school programs since its inception in 2003. Glen remembers going to a Math Games event sponsored by his third-grade daughter's elementary school—involving a simple set of activities for parents and children to do together at home, such as estimating how many cotton balls were in a jar. It was engaging and fun, and introduced ideas for home learning.

Children perform better academically when fathers and mothers become involved in school as well as help with homework.[44] There are many opportunities for fathers to get involved in their child's school. They can attend school events, volunteer in the classroom, and join parent organizations. Some fathers feel uncomfortable with volunteering in the classroom, but teachers greatly appreciate fathers who volunteer. A good first step is simply to ask teachers if there is some way that they can help.

A number of researchers have found that school personnel are not as open to father involvement as they are to mother involvement. Rema Reynolds and colleagues interviewed 16 Black fathers about their perceptions of school involvement.[45] The most consistent theme mentioned by fathers was their perception that staff were uncomfortable with their presence in the school. The fathers told interviewers that staff appeared shocked, confused, and surprised when they were present in the school. The fathers further stated that their presence was questioned and viewed with suspicion when they made efforts to engage with staff. Research with Black fathers supports the conclusion that schools should do more to engage fathers.

## Social Development

Earlier in this chapter, we wrote about children's social–emotional competence. A major component of this competence includes children's cooperative and prosocial behaviors and their ability to initiate and maintain friendships.[46] Children who have friends, engage in prosocial behaviors, and are accepted by peers tend to have higher overall well-being and school success.[47] Parents facilitate children's social competence by providing opportunities for children to interact with peers. For example, they arrange children's play dates, plan activities such as birthday parties and outings with peers, and accompany children to the playground. Fathers provide children with access to social opportunities through religious institutions, initiating informal contact with peers, and signing up children for formal after-school activities such as team sports.[48] Fathers who provide these social opportunities for their school-age children are more likely to have socially competent children.[49] However, fathers are not always able to arrange social opportunities for children because of their work schedules. The Afterschool Alliance conducted a national household survey of nearly 30,000 families in 2009 to learn how many children were in after-school programs and how many were unsupervised after school.[50] The study found that 4% of elementary school children are unsupervised after school until their parents return from work. Although after-school activities are an important source of socialization for children, they are not always realistic for many families.

Fathers also influence children's prosocial behavior with peers by modeling effective problem-solving and conflict resolution. These parental interactions are more likely to occur when fathers are nurturant and responsive to their children and when they use less authoritarian behavioral control strategies (i.e., less rigid and conflicted interactions with children). Fathers who respond positively, encourage independence, and engage in problem-solving during discussions about difficult issues are more likely to have school-age children with higher levels of social competence.[51] Children are more likely to seek out their fathers for help with friendship problems when fathers listen attentively and encourage problem-solving. Children who are exposed to positive parenting from fathers learn to solve their own problems with peers. They also learn that their perspective on a dispute may be different from another person's perspective. Understanding that there are different perspectives helps children to reach compromises.

Fathers also influence children's social competence by providing instruction about effective strategies for interacting with peers. For example, they may suggest ways that children can appropriately express their likes and dislikes when friends want to engage in certain activities. They encourage children to be sensitive to others and not just go along with the group, and they encourage children to stand up for themselves and avoid becoming involved in anything that feels wrong or they do not like, including roleplaying what the child might do or say in those situations. Elementary-age children are more socially competent when fathers provide sensitive and warm advice about peer interactions.[52]

## Challenging Issues during Middle Childhood

Parenting challenges are universal. The Pew Research Center conducted a national survey of 3,757 U.S. parents with children under age 18 and found that 24% of fathers and 33% of mothers reported that parenting is stressful at least most of the time.[53] The two most common concerns expressed by parents were children being bullied and children's anxiety and depression.

**Bullying.** Bullying is defined as "any unwanted aggressive behavior(s) by other youth or groups of youths who are not siblings or current dating partners that involves an observed or perceived power imbalance and is repeated multiple times or is highly likely to be repeated."[54] Children may be victims or perpetrators of bullying. Bullying victimization occurs most often at the end of middle childhood and the beginning of adolescence (ages 11 to 13), and perpetration occurs most often between ages 12 and 14.[55] However, children may experience bullying at earlier ages. There are many reasons why children bully their peers. For example, children model aggressive behavior towards others that they witness at home. When children witness aggressive fathers or mothers they develop the expectation that behaving aggressively has the benefit of getting attention or getting your way.[56] Children who experience family violence are more likely to be perpetrators or victims of bullying.[57] Bullying can also increase children's popularity with their peers. Some children bully because of peer pressure. Higher levels of parental support towards children, positive family relationships, parental engagement in schools, and parent's knowledge of bullying are associated with lower peer bullying and victimization. There are many resources available to fathers to help children stop bullying or being bullied. The American Psychological Association recommends steps to address bullying (see Text Box 6.4), including teaching children to be assertive and stand up to bullies. Children should also understand that reporting to adults about bullies can help to stop the bully's attacks.

---

**TEXT BOX 6.4**

**How Parents Can Take Action to Prevent Bullying**

Parents of kids being bullied:

- Observe your child for signs they might be being bullied
- Teach your child how to handle being bullied
- Set boundaries with technology to help prevent online bullying

Parents of kids engaged in bullying:

- Stop bullying before it starts by educating children about bullying
- Make your home "bully free" by limiting overly strict or aggressive behaviors
- Look for self-esteem issues

Source: Adapted from American Psychological Association, https://www.apa.org/topics/bullying/prevent.

**Depression.** It is often assumed that children do not experience depression in middle childhood, but they do. School-aged children experience hormone fluctuations for the first time, get pressure from peers that can cause anxiety, and are disappointed when they do not perform as they expect or as well as their peers.[58] About 3% of children experience clinical depression and 10% of children report occasional sadness and depression during middle childhood.[59] Clinical depression (sometimes called Major Depressive Disorder) refers to symptoms such as sadness, feelings of worthlessness, and lack of energy (just to name a few) that are severe enough to cause noticeable problems in social relationships and in day-to-day activities, such as school or social activities. Nearly all children experience occasional feelings of sadness or melancholy, but that does not mean they are clinically depressed. Children tend to report more depression as they approach adolescence. Rates of depression among 12-year-olds are higher than at almost any other age during childhood and adolescence.[60] Boys experience more depression than girls during middle childhood. That trend reverses during adolescence. The Covid-19 pandemic took a great toll on children's mental health, with some children still experiencing those effects. Researchers have found that worldwide rates of depression and anxiety doubled during the pandemic.[61] Although depression and anxiety were most prevalent among adolescents, they also occurred at alarmingly high rates among younger children.

There are many possible causes of childhood depression. Many studies have shown that depression tends to run in families. Other factors that contribute to depression include illness, child temperament, low peer acceptance, having few friends, school failure, family stress, harsh parenting, developmental changes, learned helplessness, and poor coping responses.[62] Fathers' relationships with children play an important role in preventing childhood depression. Jia Yan and colleagues found that fathers who have closer relationships with sons and daughters (e.g., share affectionate, warm relationships with their children) during grades 1–5 have children who report less depression than children whose fathers do not share close relationships with them.[63]

Extreme depression can lead to suicidal thoughts and behaviors in children. It is important for fathers and mothers to speak with their child's primary health care provider or a mental health specialist if they suspect their child has depression. Parents may also consider contacting the 988 Lifeline, which is available 24 hours a day, 7 days a week in the United States for free. Lifeline provides confidential emotional support to people in suicidal crisis or emotional distress; the caller can check that they are concerned with "someone else's safety" to talk about a child in crisis.

**Learning Challenges.** The National Center for Learning Disabilities reported that one in five children had learning or attention challenges in the 2015–2016 school year.[64] The most common types of learning challenges are "specific learning disabilities," such as dyslexia[65]—significant difficulty learning to read. There are other specific learning disabilities, including perceptual challenges, math disability, writing disability, and others. Having a child with learning challenges can be stressful for fathers, who may not know how to support their children's learning. Children with learning challenges often learn new material differently than other children. For example, some children are auditory learners—they learn better by hearing and listening than by reading. It is important for fathers to work closely with teachers and other school staff to learn how to assist children's learning. Schools are required to provide resources for children with learning challenges. However, schools in the United States vary widely in the extent to which they offer these resources. In addition, parents do not always agree with school staff about the best way to meet their children's needs. Many parents find that they have to advocate in order to obtain the appropriate resources to support their children's learning. Fathers and mothers may seek out resources outside of the school to enhance their children's learning. These resources can be costly and are not accessible to all parents.

Fathers may also experience stress when children become frustrated with learning new material or completing homework. Some children progress through several grades in school before it is determined that they have a learning challenge. Children may hear from teachers that they are completing a task incorrectly or that they need to listen better. Over time children may start to feel inadequate or stupid. It is very important for fathers to listen for these feelings in children because they may indicate the presence of a learning challenge that, if unaddressed, can have negative long-term consequences for children's self-esteem and performance in school.

One of the most challenging issues experienced by children is attention deficit hyperactivity disorder, also known as ADHD. ADHD is a neurodevelopmental disorder characterized by symptoms of inattention, hyperactivity, and/or impulsivity that cause impairment in multiple settings.[66] Dr. Russell Barkley, who is one of the foremost experts on ADHD in the United States, has argued that this disorder is more about difficulties with self-regulation than it is about inattention or hyperactivity.[67] In fact, he refers to the disorder as "self-regulation deficit disorder." According to Barkley, children's difficulties are primarily with self-restraint, emotional self-regulation, self-motivation, and behavioral self-regulation. Children with ADHD can be very impulsive and can have difficulty with persisting at tasks, organizing, and planning. They may also have difficulty with maintaining friendships and getting along with peers. Fathers often struggle to cope with children with ADHD. These children place many more demands on fathers' time and attention than other children. Children's impulsivity, lack of self-restraint, and lack of emotional and behavioral self-regulation can challenge parents to stay calm with children who often appear out of control and are disobedient. Fathers need to understand that children's behaviors are largely the result of differences in the development of the prefrontal cortex in the brain, that is, the executive functioning part of the brain.

ADHD tends to run in families, although the exact genetic cause of ADHD is not well understood. Children with ADHD may have fathers, mothers, aunts, or uncles with a history of ADHD. All children need consistent discipline and support to grow into healthy adolescents and adults. Consistent discipline and support are especially important for children with self-regulation challenges. Fathers who have a history of ADHD may be highly reactive to their children's lack of self-regulation, thus making the challenge of parenting especially difficult.[68] Children with ADHD do much better when fathers and mothers learn about the disorder and receive support. The American Academy of Child and Adolescent Psychiatry has an excellent website with many resources for parents (www.aacap.org/AACAP/Families _and_Youth/Resource_Centers/ADHD_Resource_Center/Home .aspx).[69] The Academy suggests that treatment for ADHD is most effective when it begins early and is individualized to the needs of the child.

**Nonresident Fathers.** We have described the challenges of being a father when one does not live with children throughout this book. Many nonresident fathers divorced the children's mother. Divorced fathers may have joint physical custody of their children and reside with their children about half the time or for more limited amounts of time. A much smaller number of divorced fathers have sole custody of children and reside with their children all of the time. Fathers have to make many adjustments when they are divorced, including establishing new patterns of involvement with children. There may be discord between divorced fathers and mothers. Conflict can lead to fathers struggling to stay involved with their children, especially if the mother engages in gatekeeping. In Chapter 3, we defined gatekeeping as mothers' preferences and decisions to handle child-related matters themselves rather than sharing childcare and decisions with fathers.

Children become more independent from their parents in middle childhood and may not want to miss play dates, sports events, or birthday parties even though they are scheduled to be with their father. It is important for divorced fathers to stay involved with children during this stage of development, but it is also important to support the children's independent social lives when possible. Not staying involved may result in fathers having more distant relationships with children as time goes on. Fathers who have become emotionally and physically distanced from children in middle childhood may find that staying involved with children is even more challenging during adolescence because children's lives center to an even greater extent outside of the family. Jay has conducted research on father–child relationships in middle childhood and adolescent depression. He has found that 15-year-olds who do not reside with their fathers report less depression when they have close relationships with nonresident fathers at age 9. Jay's study highlights the importance of divorced fathers maintaining close relationships with their school-age children.

Divorced fathers frequently desire to have close relationships with their children but are faced with significant barriers to maintaining contact. Maternal gatekeeping is not the only barrier that some divorced fathers face. They frequently lack support from family members and friends. Workplace demands may conflict with their scheduled days and times for being with children. Child custody laws still do a poor job of ensuring that fathers have equal access to children. Child support is an important source of financial support for children, but many fathers (especially low-income fathers) have difficulty meeting their support obligations. These fathers may owe more and more money as time goes by. Nonpayment of child support often leads to conflict between mothers and fathers, with mothers feeling that fathers are not being responsible parents.

There are a growing number of community supports for fathers, although not all communities have such supports available. One such group is Fathers for Families of Pennsylvania, which helps separated and divorced fathers to navigate the challenging process of separation and divorce (dadsrc.org/fathers -for-families/). The adult children of divorced parents have told Jay and Glen that their fathers infrequently took them to visit relatives, including cousins, aunts, uncles, and grandparents. They missed out on those relationships and on important information about the family that they might otherwise have had. Divorced fathers should take children to visit their extended family, keep them in touch with them, and encourage relationships with their kin.

## Summary

Middle childhood is a joyful time for fathers. Although children are becoming more independent and spend more time away from home, they are still very much involved in the family. They like spending time with fathers and look up to them as role models. This is an important time for fathers to support children's healthy living, learning in school, and emotional and social development. The rewards include a closer father–child relationship, learning with your child, and having fun together. Children and fathers grow and develop in important ways when fathers are actively engaged with children.

## Notes

1 Huston, A. C., & Ripke, M. N. (2006). *Developmental contexts in middle childhood: Bridges to adolescence and adulthood*. Cambridge University Press.
2 Livingston, G. (2018). *Most dads say they spend too little time with their children; about a quarter live apart from them*. Pew Research Center. www.pewresearch .org/short-reads/2018/01/08/most-dads-say-they-spend-too-little-time -with-their-children-about-a-quarter-live-apart-from-them/
3 Greenhaus, H. J., Collins, M. K., & Shaw, D. J. (2003). The relation between work–family balance and quality of life. *Journal of Vocational Behaviour, 63*, 510–531, p. 513. https://doi.org/10.1016/S0001-8791(02)00042-8
4 Fagan, J., & Press, J. (2008). Father influences on employed mothers' work–family balance. *Journal of Family Issues, 29*, 1136–1160. https://doi.org/10.1177 /0192513X07311954
5 Nomaguchi, K., & Johnson, W. (2016). Parenting stress among low-income and working-class fathers: The role of employment. *Journal of Family Issues, 37*(11), 1535–1557. https://doi.org/10.1177/0192513X14560642
6 Bronfenbrenner, U., & Morris, P. A. (2006). The bioecological model of human development. In W. Damon & R. M. Lerner (Eds.), *Handbook of child psychology, vol. 1: Theoretical models of human development* (6th ed., pp. 793–828). Wiley.
7 McHale, J. P., Kuersten-Hogan, R., & Rao, N. (2004). Growing points for coparenting theory and research. *Journal of Adult Development, 11*, 221–234. https://doi.org/10.1023/B:JADE.0000035629.29960.ed
8 Lewis, C., & Lamb, M. E. (2003). Fathers' influences on children's development: The evidence from two-parent families. *European Journal of Psychology of Education, 18*(2), 211–228. https://doi.org/10.1007/BF03173485
9 Cabrera, N. J., Volling, B. L., & Barr, R. (2018). Fathers are parents, too! Widening the lens on parenting for children's development. *Child Development Perspectives, 12*, 152–157. https://doi.org/10.1111/cdep.12275
10 Cabrera, N. J., Volling, B. L., & Barr, R. (2018). Fathers are parents, too!; Lewis, C., & Lamb, M. E. (2003). Fathers' influences on children's development.

11 Fagan, J. (2022). Longitudinal associations among low-income mothers' and fathers' parenting and relationships with children and adolescent depression. *Research on Child and Adolescent Psychopathology, 50*(10), 1339–1350. https://doi.org/10.1007/s10802-022-00918-0

12 Paris, J., Ricardo, A., & Rymond, D. (2019). *Child growth and development*. College of the Canyons.

13 Litchford, A., Savoie Roskos, M. R., & Wengreen, H. (2020). Influence of fathers on the feeding practices and behaviors of children: A systematic review. *Appetite, 147*, 104558. https://doi.org/10.1016/j.appet.2019.104558

14 Tschann, J. M., Gregorich, S. E., Penilla, C. Pasch, L. A., de Groat, C. L., Flores, E., Deardorff, J., Greenspan, L. C., & Butte, N. F.(2013). Parental feeding practices in Mexican American families: Initial test of an expanded measure. *International Journal of Behavioral Nutrition and Physical Activity, 10*(6). https://doi.org/10.1186/1479-5868-10-6; Watterworth, J. C., Hutchinson, J. M., Buchholz, A. C., Darlington, G., Randall Simpson, J. A., Ma, D. W. L., & Haines, J. (2017). Food parenting practices and their association with child nutrition risk status: Comparing mothers and fathers. *Applied Physiology, Nutrition and Metabolism, 42*(6), 667–671. https://doi.org/10.1139/apnm-2016-0572

15 Parada, H., Ayala, G. X., Horton, L. A., Ibarra, L., & Arredondo, E. M. (2016). Latino fathers' feeding-related parenting strategies on children's eating. *Ecology of Food and Nutrition, 55*(3), 292–307. https://doi.org/10.1080/03670244.2016.1161616

16 Rahill, S., Kennedy, A., & Kearney, J. (2020). A review of the influence of fathers on children's eating behaviours and dietary intake. *Appetite, 147*, 104540. https://doi.org/10.1016/j.appet.2019.104540

17 Rahill, S., Kennedy, A., & Kearney, J. (2020). A review of the influence of fathers.

18 Khandpur, N., et al. (2016). Diversity in fathers' food parenting practices: A qualitative exploration within a heterogeneous sample. *Appetite, 101*, 134–145. https://doi.org/10.1016/j.appet.2016.02.161; Walsh, A. D., Hesketh, K. D., van der Pligt, P., Cameron, A. J., Crawford, D., & Campbell, K. J. (2017). Fathers' perspectives on the diets and physical activity behaviours of their young children. *PloS One Public Library of Science, 12*(6), e0179210. https://doi.org/10.1371/journal.pone.0179210

19 Loughborough University Child Feeding Guide. (2017). *Children not seeing others role modeling*. www.childfeedingguide.co.uk/tips/common-feeding-pitfalls/role-modelling/

20 Biddle, S. J. H., Ciaccioni, S., Thomas, G., & Vergeer, I. (2019). Physical activity and mental health in children and adolescents: An updated review of reviews and an analysis of causality. *Psychology of Sport and Exercise, 42*,146–155. https://doi.org/10.1016/j.psychsport.2018.08.011; Vannatta, K., Gartstein, M. A., Zeller, M., & Noll, R. B. (2009). Peer acceptance and social behavior during childhood and adolescence: How important are appearance, athleticism, and academic competence? *International Journal of Behavioral Development, 33*(4), 303–311. https://doi.org/10.1177/0165025408101275; Wyszyńska, J., Ring-Dimitriou, S., Thivel, D., Weghuber, D., Hadjipanayis, A., Grossman, Z., Ross-Russell, R., Dereń, K., & Mazur, A. (2020). Physical activity in the prevention of childhood obesity: The position of the European Childhood Obesity Group and the European Academy of Pediatrics. *Frontiers in Pediatrics, 8*, 535705. https://www.frontiersin.org/articles/10.3389/fped.2020.535705

21 Coakley, J. (2006). The good father: Parental expectations and youth sports. *Leisure Studies, 25*(2), 153–163. https://doi.org/10.1080/02614360500467735

22 Jeanes, R., & Magee, J. (2011). Come on my son! Examining fathers, masculinity and "fathering through football." *Annals of Leisure Research, 14*(2–3), 273–288. https://doi.org/10.1080/11745398.2011.616483

23 Matos, R., Monteiro, D., Amaro, N., Antunes, R., Coelho, L., Mendes, D., & Arufe-Giráldez, V. (2021). Parents' and children's (6–12 years old) physical activity association: A systematic review from 2001 to 2020. *International Journal of Environmental Research and Public Health, 18*(23), 12651. https://doi.org/10.3390/ijerph182312651

24 Matos, R., Monteiro, D., Amaro, N., Antunes, R., Coelho, L., Mendes, D., & Arufe-Giráldez, V. (2021). Parents' and children's (6–12 years old) physical activity association.

25 Edwardson, C. L., & Gorely, T. (2010). Activity-related parenting practices and children's objectively measured physical activity. *Pediatric Exercise Science, 22*(1), 105–113. https://doi.org/10.1123/pes.22.1.105

26 Neshteruk, C. D., Nezami, B. T., Nino-Tapias, G., Davison, K. K., & Ward, D. S. (2017). The influence of fathers on children's physical activity: A review of the literature from 2009 to 2015. *Preventive Medicine, 102*, 12–19. https://doi.org/10.1016/j.ypmed.2017.06.027

27 Denham, S. A., Salich, M., Olthof, T., Kochanoff, A., & Caverly, S. (2004). Emotional and social development in childhood. In P. K. Smith & C. H. Hart (Eds.), *Childhood social development* (pp. 307–328). Blackwell.

28 Fosco, G. M., & Grych, J. H. (2012). Capturing the family context of emotion regulation: A family systems model comparison approach. *Journal of Family Issues, 34*(4), 557–578. https://doi.org/10.1177/0192513X12445889; Sosa-Hernandez, S., Sack, L., Seddon, J. A., Bailey, K., & Thomassin, K. (2020). Mother and father repertoires of emotion socialization practices in middle childhood. *Journal of Applied Developmental Psychology, 69*, 101159. https://doi.org/10.1016/j.appdev.2020.101159; Thomassin, K., & Suveg, C. (2014). Reciprocal positive affect and well-regulated, adjusted children: A unique contribution of fathers. *Parenting, 14*(1), 28–46. https://doi.org/10.1080/15295192.2014.880017

29 Wang, M., Wang, Y., Wang, F., & Xing, X. (2021). Parental corporal punishment and child temperament: Independent and interactive predictors of child emotion regulation in China. *Journal of Interpersonal Violence, 36*(11–12), 6680–6698. https://doi.org/10.1177/0886260518817058

30 Sosa-Hernandez, S., Sack, L., Seddon, J. A., Bailey, K., & Thomassin, K. (2020). Mother and father repertoires of emotion socialization; Morris, A. S., Criss, M. M., Silk, J. S., & Houltberg, B. J. (2017). The impact of parenting on emotion regulation during childhood and adolescence. *Child Development Perspectives, 11*, 233–238. http://dx.doi.org/10.1111/cdep.12238

31 Carr, A. (2017). Social and emotional development in middle childhood. In D. Skuse, H. Bruce, & L. Dowdney (Eds.), *Child psychology and psychiatry*. Wiley. https://doi.org/10.1002/9781119170235.ch10

32 Paris, J., Ricardo, A., & Rymond, D. (2019). *Child growth and development*.

33 Brumaire, L., & Kerns, K. (2010). Parent–child attachment and internalizing symptoms in childhood and adolescence: A review of empirical findings and future directions. *Development and Psychopathology, 22*(1), 177–203. https://doi.org/10.1017/S0954579409990344

34 Felson, R. B., & Zielinski, M. A. (1989). Children's self-esteem and parental support. *Journal of Marriage and Family, 51*(3), 727–735. https://doi.org/10.2307/352171

35 Khaleque, A. (2017). Perceived parental hostility and aggression, and children's psychological maladjustment, and negative personality dispositions:

A meta-analysis. *Journal of Child and Family Studies, 26*, 977–988. https://doi .org/10.1007/s10826-016-0637-9

36 Bureau, J.-F., Deneault, A.-A., & Yurkowski, K. (2020). Preschool father–child attachment and its relation to self-reported child socioemotional adaptation in middle childhood. *Attachment & Human Development, 22*(1), 90–104. https://doi.org/10.1080/14616734.2019.1589065

37 Weir, K. (2023). *How to help kids understand and manage their emotions.* American Psychological Association. https://www.apa.org/topics/parent ing/emotion-regulation

38 Paris, J., Ricardo, A., & Rymond, D. (2019). *Child growth and development.*

39 Gauvain, M. (2018). Cognitive development. In M. H. Borenstein (Ed.), *The Sage encyclopedia of lifespan human development.* https://doi.org/10.4135 /9781506307633

40 Kim, S. W., & Hill, N. E. (2015). Including fathers in the picture: A meta-analysis of parental involvement and students' academic achievement. *Journal of Educational Psychology.*http://dx.doi.org/10.1037/edu0000023

41 Kim, S. W., & Hill, N. E. (2015). Including fathers in the picture.

42 Kim, S. W., & Hill, N. E. (2015). Including fathers in the picture.

43 Strong Fathers Strong Families. (n.d.). www.strongfathers.com

44 Kim, S. W., & Hill, N. E. (2015). Including fathers in the picture.

45 Reynolds, R. E., Howard, T. C., & Kenyatta Jones, T. (2015). Is this what educators really want? Transforming the discourse on Black fathers and their participation in schools. *Race Ethnicity and Education, 18*(1), 89–107. https:// doi.org/10.1080/13613324.2012.759931

46 Squires, J. (2003). *The importance of early identification of social and emotional difficulties in preschool children.* Center for International Rehabilitation. https://eip.uoregon.edu/asqse/pdf/ImportEarly_IdenCIR.pdf

47 Taylor, R. D., Oberle, E., Durlak, J. A., & Weissberg, R. P. (2017). Promoting positive youth development through school-based social and emotional learning interventions: A meta-analysis of follow-up effects. *Child Development, 88*(4), 1156–1171. https://doi.org/10.1111/cdev.12864

48 Leidy, M. S., Schofield, T. J., & Parke, R. D. (2013). Fathers' contributions to children's social development. In N. J. Cabrera & C. S. Tamis-LeMonda (Eds.), *Handbook of father involvement: Multidisciplinary perspectives* (pp. 151–167). Routledge/Taylor & Francis Group.

49 McDowell, D. J., & Parke, R. D. (2009). Parental correlates of children's peer relations: An empirical test of a tripartite model. *Developmental Psychology, 45*(1), 224. https://doi.org/10.1037/a0014305

50 Afterschool Alliance. (n.d.). *America after 3 pm.* afterschoolalliance.org/d ocuments/aa3pm_key_findings_2009.pdf

51 McDowell, D. J., Kim, M., O'Neil, R., & Parke, R. D. (2002). Children's emotional regulation and social competence in middle childhood. *Marriage & Family Review, 34*(3–4), 345–364. https://doi.org/10.1300/J002v34n03_07

52 Leidy, M. S., Schofield, T. J., & Parke, R. D. (2013). Fathers' contributions to children's social development; McDowell, D. J., & Parke, R. D. (2009). Parental correlates of children's peer relations.

53 Minkin, R., & Horowitz, J. M. (2023). *Parenting in America today.* www .pewresearch.org/social-trends/2023/01/24/parenting-in-america-today/

54 Gladden, R. M., Vivolo-Kantor, A. M., Hamburger M. E., & Lumpkin C. D. (2014). *Bullying surveillance among youths: Uniform definitions for public health and recommended data elements, version 1.0.* (p. 7). Centers for Disease Control and Prevention. https://www.cdc.gov/violenceprevention/pdf/bullying -definitions-final-a.pdf

55 Finkelhor, D., Turner, H. A., Shattuck, A., & Hamby S. L. (2015). Prevalence of childhood exposure to violence, crime, and abuse: Results from the national survey of children's exposure to violence. *JAMA Pediatrics, 169*(8), 746–754. https://doi.org/10.1001/jamapediatrics.2015.0676

56 de Vries, E. E., Verlinden, M., Rijlaarsdam, J., Jaddoe, V. W. V., Verhulst, F. V., Arseneault, L., & Tiemeier, H. (2018). Like father, like child: Early life family adversity and children's bullying behaviors in elementary school. *Journal of Abnormal Child Psychology, 46,*1481–1496. https://doi.org/10.1007/s10802-017 -0380-8

57 Yoon, J., Bauman, S., & Corcoran, C. (2020). Role of adults in prevention and intervention of peer victimization. In L. H. Rosen, S. R. Scott, & S. Y. Kim (Eds.), *Bullies, victims, and bystanders.* Palgrave Macmillan. https://doi.org /10.1007/978-3-030-52939-0_7

58 Yan, J., Schoppe-Sullivan, S. J., & Feng, X. (2019). Trajectories of mother–child and father–child relationships across middle childhood and associations with depressive symptoms. *Development and Psychopathology, 31*(4), 1381–1393.

59 Garber, J., & Rao, U. (2014). Depression in children and adolescents. In M. Lewis & K. D. Ruldolph (Eds.), *Handbook of developmental psychopathology* (pp. 489–520). Springer.

60 Twenge, J. M., & Nolen-Hoeksema, S. (2002). Age, gender, race, socioeconomic status, and birth cohort difference on the children's depression inventory: A meta-analysis. *Journal of Abnormal Psychology, 111*, 578–588. https://doi.org/10.1037/0021-843X.111.4.578

61 Racine, N., McArthur, B. A., Cooke, J. E., Eirich, R., Zhu, J., & Madigan, S. (2021). Global prevalence of depressive and anxiety symptoms in children and adolescents during COVID-19: A meta-analysis. *JAMA Pediatrics, 175*(11), 1142–1150. https://doi.org/10.1001/jamapediatrics.2021.2482

62 Malhotra, S., & Sahoo, S. (2018). Antecedents of depression in children and adolescents. *Indian Psychiatry Journal, 27*(1), 11–16. https://doi.org/10.4103/ ipj.ipj_29_17

63 Yan, J., Schoppe-Sullivan, S. J., & Feng, X. (2019). Trajectories of mother–child and father–child relationships.

64 National Center for Learning Disabilities. (2017). *Snapshot of learning and attention issues in the U.S.* https://ncld.org/wp-content/uploads/2017/03/1 -in-5-Snapshot.Fin_.03142017.pdf

65 Schaeffer, K. (2023). *What federal education data shows about students with disabilities in the U.S.* Pew Research Center. www.pewresearch.org/short-reads /2023/07/24/what-federal-education-data-shows-about-students-with-dis- abilities-in-the-us/

66 American Psychiatric Association. (2013). *Diagnostic and statistical manual of mental disorders* (5th ed.). Author.

67 Barkley, R. A. (2022). *Treating ADHD in children and adolescents.* Guilford.

68 Mokrova, I., O'Brien, M., Calkins, S., & Keane, S. (2010). Parental ADHD symptomology and ineffective parenting: The connecting link of home chaos. *Parenting, 10*(2), 119–135. https://doi.org/10.1080/15295190903212844

69 American Academy of Child and Adolescent Psychiatry. (n.d.). ADHD resource center. www.aacap.org/AACAP/Families_and_Youth/Resource _Centers/ADHD_Resource_Center/Home.aspx

# Fathers and Adolescents

## Exploring Identities and Expanding Social Relationships

*I think what I like the most [about having teenagers] ... is that they are truly coming into their own. When I have conversations with them, it is like having conversations with coequals. They have their own thoughts, their own perceptions on things, which are important aspects of the growth process for them and for us. That's the thing I like the most. Just getting to know them as people. We've spent a lot of time with them growing up, giving them good values. Now we get to see how they are implementing [those values] in their day-to-day lives. ... I love coming home and talking to them about their day. ... I have an 18- and 17-year-old. The 18-year-old is a much more independent thinker. The 13-year-old, sometimes you need to prod her a little bit. But that's the part I enjoy the most about them at this age.*

*[Most challenging is that] as they grow up and come into their own, sometimes you have to say as a parent, be willing to say, that may not be the choice I would make or the way I would approach things. But giving them the space to be able to grow in that a little bit. That comes across in any number of areas. Having older children, it was most apparent when they started to drive. Giving them the freedom to understand this is a big responsibility and not constantly watching them on ... "find my iPhone." ... There is a big trust factor. Not because they are bad kids but because you do not have as much control over what they are doing, where they are, or how they are doing it, as you did when they were younger. And hoping and relying on the fact that we instilled good values. That is the best part, and the most challenging part.*

—Father of three daughters, ages 13, 17, and 18

## Introduction

Adolescence is the longest period of childhood, lasting for about 8 years from ages 12 to 19. This is the stage of development when individuals transition from being children to being adults.

DOI: 10.4324/9781003486107-7

Adolescence typically begins with puberty, which can start as early as age 10 or 11 for girls and 11 or 12 for boys. Age of onset of puberty has declined by about three to four months per decade since the nineteenth century, due in part to better nutrition.[1]

Adolescents undergo important changes in physical and brain development, social and emotional behavior, cognitive and academic skills, and relationships with parents and other family members. Fathers must adapt to these changes to help their adolescents grow into healthy and well-adjusted young adults. At the same time, there are many environmental influences (e.g., social media) that place constraints on the influence that fathers have on their youth.

Fathers and mothers spend less time with their children as children grow older. This is largely because children become more independent during adolescence and because children's focus shifts from the family to peers, school, and activities such as sports, music, and dance.[2] However, this is not to say that fathers are any less important or influential than they were during their children's earlier years. In fact, children can develop significant emotional or behavioral problems when fathers (and mothers) do not stay closely involved with them through their teen years.

This chapter addresses the developmental tasks of fathers who have adolescent children. The chapter also describes important developmental tasks of children during adolescence. A key task is to develop a coherent sense of self and identity. These tasks explain an adolescents' motivations as they interact with their family and the larger world. The chapter will also address several challenges that contemporary fathers face: adolescent alcohol and drug use and social media use.

## Developmental Tasks of Fathers during Adolescence

A central challenge for fathers is to adapt to adolescents' motivation to make independent decisions and experiment with new behaviors, roles, and relationships.[3] The shift toward greater experimentation and autonomy takes place in the context of adolescents' shift from focusing on family to focusing on peers. By experimenting, adolescents learn about their capacity to make autonomous decisions, but they typically overvalue the benefits and undervalue the risks of activities.[4] These tendencies make adolescents vulnerable to engaging in risky behaviors such as delinquency and drug abuse. These shifts in adolescent behavior can be challenging for fathers who must find a balance between supporting children's desire for independence and ensuring their safety. During late adolescence, fathers must adapt to their children's decisions about education or vocational training, entry into and transitions within the labor market, moving out of the family home, and sometimes marriage and parenthood.[5] The father quoted at the beginning of this chapter clearly articulated these challenges with finding a balance:

> *I think the hardest part for me was always being patient and understanding and empathetic of someone else's positions. That was hard for me when I was growing up. It is something I've developed. I am certainly no expert in it ... , but that is the thing I've seen the most growth, in being more patient, willing to listen, being more understanding, but having to be firm at the right times. Frankly the challenge that I have is dealing with when those times are ... when is the right time to be challenging and when is the right time to be more understanding and allowing them to go down whatever path they want to choose, even if that path I can see is not going to end well, but letting them make their own mistake.*

Most fathers adapt well to changes in their children. That is, they find an appropriate balance between supporting children's strivings for independence and ensuring their safety. However, some fathers find it more difficult to adapt. Judith Smetana has suggested that much of the conflict between parents and adolescents is due to different beliefs and expectations about adolescents' behavior.[6] Adolescents tend to value personal choice and autonomy whereas parents value safety, responsibility, and adherence to social norms (e.g., saying "hello" to neighbors). Fathers may feel nostalgic for their younger child, who always wanted to spend time with them and who idolized and wanted to be just like them. In their striving for autonomy, adolescents may conceal information from fathers, not want to spend time in family activities, talk back to parents when they feel their autonomy is being threatened, break rules such as curfews, and not tell fathers where they are going and with whom. Some fathers adapt to these changes by becoming overly permissive with children. Other fathers may become more authoritarian, that is, rigidly expecting obedience and compliance without question. Fathers who are too authoritarian may find that there is growing conflict with their adolescent. Conflict that is too frequent may push children away so that they become less communicative with their fathers and want to spend less time at home. Fathers who are too permissive may find that their children engage in higher levels of risky behavior.

## Communication Challenges

A significant challenge for fathers during adolescence is to maintain a close and communicative relationship with their child while giving the child increasing autonomy. Several studies have found that fathers report becoming closer to their children during the transition to adolescence compared with earlier years.[7] However, studies of father–daughter relationships have shown that daughters report feeling less comfortable communicating with fathers during adolescence.[8] They are also likely to feel that talking with mothers is more beneficial than talking with fathers.[9] Rachel Blickman and Cynthia Campbell have suggested that fathers communicate less with daughters during adolescence because they undervalue the unique contributions they make to their daughter's healthy development.[10] Fathers and daughters who report having better communication with each other express greater feelings of relationship satisfaction.[11] Fathers' relationships with sons are also important. Youth who report closer relationships with fathers have fewer mental health problems and better self-rated health.[12]

Fathers' ability to adapt to the changing developmental needs of adolescents can be negatively affected by fathers' exposure to stress, such as workplace demands, poverty, conflict with one's partner, and their own memories of childhood adversity.[13]

A recent national survey of fathers and mothers with adolescent children indicated that 15% of fathers reported anxiety and 10% of fathers reported depressive symptoms.[14] Fathers' anxiety and depression can negatively affect their important ability to be attuned to their adolescents' needs. Fathers can be attuned to their adolescents by being positively engaged with their children, monitoring and supervising behavior, and engaging in open communication.[15] We discuss this further in this chapter. Here are several questions for fathers to reflect on as ways to think about adolescence.

## Reflection Questions

- ◆ How has your upbringing influenced the way in which you are raising your adolescent?
- ◆ What are your biggest challenges adapting to your child's strivings for independence?
- ◆ How has your relationship with your child changed since the onset of adolescence?
- ◆ How easy is it for you and your adolescent to communicate with one another?
- ◆ How is your own mental health and how is this impacting your relationship with your adolescent?

## Coparenting Challenges

Maintaining a healthy coparenting relationship with the child's mother is crucial during adolescence. Parents are the main source of support as children go through adolescence. Fathers and mothers who do not support and communicate effectively with each other about their parenting practices and about the adolescent may find that that they are less able to support their child. A number of potential coparenting issues can arise. Some fathers were given a good deal of freedom when they were growing up. They may feel that their adolescent should also be allowed to have those freedoms. Some fathers had parents who were strict and expected children to be obedient. These fathers may feel that the strict restrictions placed on them while growing up should not be placed on their own children, or they may emulate their own parents and expect exact obedience from children. Fathers' beliefs about how to raise an adolescent can conflict with the mothers' belief when parents have different views about monitoring children's behavior and setting rules. Adolescents easily perceive their parents' differences and may try to exploit them. For example, adolescents may challenge parents' protectiveness by saying that one parent allows them to stay out late or go places that are forbidden by the other parent. Making decisions about how much independence to give adolescents can be challenging when children are exposed to social media influences or have friends whose parents are overly permissive.

Parents' disagreements about how much independence to give children and how much monitoring they should provide can lead to considerable conflict between them. Psychologists have found that conflict between parents can spill over into parenting practices. For example, mothers' warmth and involvement toward adolescents can be negatively impacted by fathers' conflict with the mother.[16] Fathers express more negativity towards adolescent children when there is a high level of coparenting conflict.[17] Fathers' reports of coparenting conflict are also negatively associated with adolescents' life satisfaction[18] and overall adjustment,[19] suggesting that conflict between parents not only spills over to parenting, but also spills overs to adolescent well-being.

In Chapter 1 of this book, we indicated that family systems theory is a useful framework for understanding fathers. Family systems researchers have found that families do not always adapt easily to children's transitions from one stage of development to another. Just as disagreements between parents about how to supervise and support children's independence can lead to conflict, disagreements between parents can also lead to one parent "taking sides" with their adolescent against the other parent. Family systems researchers refer to these types of relationships as family alliances or coalitions. Family alliances are not necessarily harmful, but they can become detrimental when they occur because of disagreements about raising children. When one parent takes sides with their child, the other parent is frequently viewed by the adolescent as being mean, harsh, or overprotective. Parents who form alliances with their children are likely to be viewed favorably by children when they are getting what they want, whereas the parent who is outside the alliance may be viewed negatively. The parent outside the alliance may find that they are less effective as a parent and that their relationship with the child is negatively affected. Fathers who feel caught up in these alliances may want to consider professional counseling, because the motivations for such alliances may occur at a subconscious level. A professional can help to understand family system dynamics and assist with finding a healthier balance.

## Understanding Development during Adolescence

### Physical Development

The most significant physical change during adolescence is puberty, that is, the developmental period in which hormonal changes cause significant physical changes in the body, culminating in sexual maturity.[20] The beginning phase of puberty starts with the release of the hormones testosterone in boys and estrogen and progesterone in girls. These hormones stimulate the development of the sex organs and the capacity to make babies. Secondary sex characteristics develop later, and although they are not directly linked to reproduction, they are important markers of puberty. They include the enlargement of breasts, widening of hips, and growth of body hair in girls and the appearance of facial and body hair, deepening of voice, and increased muscle mass in boys. These are just a few of the secondary sex characteristics associated with puberty.

The age of onset of puberty varies widely among boys and girls. Girls who reach puberty early (before age 8) are sometimes teased by their peers, especially if the start of puberty occurs when girls are still in elementary school. Girls can become self-conscious about reaching puberty before their peers. There is also greater risk for depression and anxiety in girls who reach puberty early, compared with later-maturing female peers.[21] Fathers are an important source of support to daughters during this stage of development. Boys who reach puberty early (before age 9), on the other hand, tend to have a positive self-image, higher self-esteem, and are more popular with their peers. Boys who mature early tend to be stronger, taller, and more athletic than their later-maturing peers, at least temporarily. These are traits that are often highly valued and may contribute to early-maturing boys' positive self-esteem.[22]

In 1982, Patricia Draper and Henry Harpending wrote a paper suggesting that girls whose fathers do not live with them experience earlier menarche (onset of menstruation) than girls whose fathers live with them.[23] This hypothesis suggested that growing up under conditions of family stress (e.g., father absence) provokes reproductive readiness because girls need to grow up faster than their peers in order to help care for the family and become self-sufficient. This hypothesis also states that girls who grow up in households where their father is present delay sexual activity because they experience higher levels of paternal investment. Although a small number of researchers found support for the influence of father absence on early puberty in girls,[24] a recent review of studies worldwide found no such support.[25]

Some evidence indicates that fathers' relationships with sons and daughters change during puberty. In a study of 122 fathers and their sons, fathers engaged in less physical affection with sons after the start of puberty.[26] There were no differences in either fathers' or sons' perceptions of companionship, support provided to the adolescent, satisfaction with the relationship, or time fathers spent with their sons. Fathers' relationships with daughters also change at the onset of puberty. Many fathers are uncomfortable talking with daughters about their physical changes and rely on mothers to have those discussions. Fathers' discomfort about talking about physical changes can lead to fathers' denial of the physical changes in their daughters.[27] The Dad University website provides excellent information about how to talk with children about puberty (see Text Box 7.1).

The child's brain undergoes dramatic changes during adolescence. It becomes more interconnected and specialized, which results in the development of more white matter. These changes enable adolescents to improve their thinking and processing skills.[28]

---

**TEXT BOX 7.1**

**Talking with Your Child about Puberty**

1. Start early—in middle childhood
2. Keep it short and simple (start with the least sensitive topics)
3. Read a book about puberty with your child
4. Use accurate names for body parts
5. Let your child ask questions
6. Use everyday situations to speak about puberty

Source: Dad University, www.youtube.com/watch?v=V-HXGvwNvRM.

---

Fathers often notice that their adolescents engage in more risk-taking and do not think through the consequences of their behavior. This occurs to some degree because the prefontal cortex does not fully mature until early adulthood. As we noted earlier in this book, the prefontal cortex is responsible for self-regulation, emotion control, planning one's actions, having foresight and hindsight, and using good judgment. Although adolescents may seem mature and adultlike in appearance, their thinking and emotional abilities are still maturing. Fathers should continue to monitor and guide their adolescent children closely and supportively because of these delays in brain development.

Children experience a growth spurt and grow taller during adolescence. Girls reach their full height at around age 16, whereas boys continue growing taller until ages 18 to 20. Staying healthy as an adolescent involves getting sufficient sleep and eating a healthy diet. The American Academy of Sleep Medicine reports that adolescents need eight to ten hours of sleep per day.[29] According to the Centers for Disease Control, fathers can help adolescents get the sleep they need by sticking to a consistent sleep schedule on weekdays and weekends and limiting light exposure and technology use in the evenings.[30] Forming healthy eating habits begins in early and middle childhood but is critical during adolescence. Children who do not eat healthy foods and exceed recommended caloric intake are at greater risk for obesity. As we discussed earlier in this book, fathers who model healthy eating and avoid restrictions on what children eat are more likely to prevent obesity in their children.

We have emphasized throughout this book the importance of children engaging in physical activity. Physical activity is often measured in studies of how individuals use their time. Few studies have focused on adolescents' daily time use in the United States. Research conducted in the United Kingdom has shown that children ages 14–16 spent significantly more time doing homework and on screens and less time in out-of-home play in 2015 compared to youth in 1975.[31] One exception was that youth spent more time participating in organized sports. These findings raise concerns about children's health. It is well-documented that low levels of physical activity are associated with obesity and lower levels of well-being. Fathers can help their adolescents by ensuring that time is allotted for self-directed play and outdoor activities while at the same time monitoring that these activities take place in safe environments.

Many children become sexually active during adolescence. According to the Centers for Disease Control, about 55% of male and female adolescents have had sexual intercourse by age 18 and approximately 80% of teens used some form of contraception at first sex.[32] Youth ages 15 to 24 represent about one half of all sexually transmitted diseases nationally. It is important for parents to talk with their children about sexual health. Fathers are less likely than mothers to communicate about sexual health with adolescent children.[33] The Centers for Disease Control provides a list of topics that parents should discuss with teens (see Text Box 7.2).[34] Parents should be aware that teens frequently learn about the *consequences* of engaging in risky behaviors in health education classes in school, but that does not take the place of conversations between parents and teens about values surrounding sexual behavior, healthy romantic relationships, respect, consent, not succumbing to peer pressure, and taking care of their sexual health.

TEXT BOX 7.2

**What Topics Should Parents Talk about with Their Teens**

♦ Talk about healthy, respectful relationships

♦ Communicate your own expectations for your teen about relationships and sex

♦ Provide factual information about ways to prevent HIV, STDs, and pregnancy (e.g., abstinence, condoms and contraception, and HIV/STD testing)

♦ Focus on the benefits of protecting oneself from HIV, STDs, and pregnancy

♦ Provide information about where your teen can speak with a provider and receive sexual health services, such as HIV/STD testing

Source: Centers for Disease Control and Prevention (n.d.), www.cdc.gov /healthyyouth/protective/factsheets/talking_teens.htm.

## Emotional Development

The physical changes that occur during adolescence occur simultaneously with significant changes in emotional development.[35] These changes include increased self-consciousness, awareness that others may be thinking about you, lack of self-confidence, a sense of vulnerability, and a fragile self-concept. There is wide variation in the degree to which adolescents experience each of these emotional changes, although nearly all adolescents experience them to some degree. Most adolescents have a strong desire to decrease their dependence on parents. At the same time adolescents may be ambivalent about their dependence on parents. That is, adolescents frequently desire independence from their parents but are at the same time reluctant to give up their dependence. For example, they may not want their fathers to monitor their homework, but they may become angry with fathers who do not help them with challenging assignments. Adolescents also tend to experience increased stress in relation to school and social demands. They can be sensitive to being evaluated by others and may feel shame when they think others are judging them negatively. Adolescents may start to doubt their ability to perform well in school, sports, get into college, and have meaningful relationships with others. These emotional developments can lead to greater depression and anxiety in adolescents.[36]

An important change during adolescence is the development of identity. The American Psychological Association defines identity as "an individual's sense of self defined by (a) a set of physical, psychological, and interpersonal characteristics that is not wholly shared with any other person and (b) a range of affiliations (e.g., ethnicity) and social roles."[37] Although identity is not wholly an emotional issue, one's identity is closely tied to sense of well-being. We indicated in Chapter 5 that important components of identity emerge during the preschool years (e.g., gender identity). Younger children possess a sense of identity that is simple and concrete. Adolescent identity is more complex and often includes the youth's commitments, personal goals, and motivations. The social aspects of identity and greater need for connection with peers become important to the way adolescents view themselves. Identities are formed through one's contact with friends, schoolmates, siblings, parents, relatives, and the wider sociocultural environment. Children are exposed to roles and expectations from these different sources, which are internalized and contribute to the adolescent's construction of identity.[38] Identity construction is an active process and involves choices made by the adolescent. Adolescents often place a lot of value in belonging to a specific identity group. Group identity is a type of social identity in which members of the group share values, beliefs, and experiences. For example, participation in sports, drama, or music activities at school can become important for identity formation of some adolescents. Forming an identity is a life-long endeavor, not a task that is completed in adolescence.[39] Identity groups can be important sources of support for adolescents as they adapt to the challenges of growing up.

Fathers influence adolescent identity development by providing a warm, secure, and supportive environment at home. Supporting adolescents' striving for autonomy and independence is important for identity development. Fathers and mothers differ somewhat in their approach to supporting adolescents' identity development. Fathers tend to encourage their maturing adolescents to engage in autonomous exploration (e.g., looking up information about careers).[40] This is less true of mothers. Mothers tend to emphasize adolescents making healthy commitments (such as making good choices regarding friends). Both autonomous exploration and making healthy commitments are important for healthy identity development.[41]

Fathers may want to reflect on the challenges that they experienced with their own identity development during adolescence to help them understand what their adolescents are experiencing. Here are a few self-reflection questions.

## Reflection Questions

◆ What were the biggest challenges that you experienced as an adolescent in developing an identity?

◆ Who were people in your life (e.g., fathers, friends, teachers) who helped you to explore your interests and strengths?

◆ How does your experience growing up help you to understand your adolescent's identity development?

Adolescence is a time when individuals begin to think of themselves more deeply in relation to their race, ethnicity, religion, gender, and sexual orientation. Youth tend to form friendships with peers from similar identity groups during the early stages of adolescence. These homogeneous social groups help youth to explore what it means to belong to a particular group. Identity development can be significantly impacted when youth are exposed to negative stereotypes based on their race, ethnicity, religion, gender, or sexual orientation. For example, Black youth in the United States are often exposed to negative stereotypes that all Blacks are violent or involved in the criminal justice system. Without support from adults, adolescents may develop negative identities or come to think negatively about being Black because of these stereotypes.[42]

Psychologists recommend that Black fathers and mothers should teach their children about what it means to be Black in the United States. Racial socialization is the process in which Black parents socialize their children about their cultural group and about mainstream society.[43] Studies have shown that racial socialization helps Black youth to develop positive beliefs about being Black and healthy identity development. Text Box 7.4 includes A. Wade Boykin and Forrest Toms' suggestions about how to engage in racial socialization.[44]

---

**TEXT BOX 7.4**

**Racial Socialization of Black Adolescents**

1. Teach children about mainstream society (e.g., what children need to know to do well in society)
2. Teach children what it means to be Black in the United States. These messages prepare them for discrimination and racism (e.g., parents inform children that they have to work harder because of their race).
3. Teach children about the Black (e.g., African American) cultural experience (e.g., discussing historical events of relevance to African Americans)

Source: From Boykin, A. W., & Toms, F. D. (1985), *Black child socialization*.

---

Some adolescents also begin to explore their gender identity and sexual orientation. The American Psychological Association defines gender as "the attitudes, feelings, and behaviors that a given culture associates with a person's biological sex."[45] In the Chapter 5, we stated that *gender identity* describes a person's psychological sense of their gender. Sexual orientation is defined as "a person's sexual and emotional attraction to another person and the behavior and/or social affiliation that may result from this attraction."[46] There are many theories about the causes of one's gender identity. Psychologists concur that gender identity develops gradually over a long period of time and is influenced by multiple factors including biological, psychological, and social factors.[47]

Finding out that their child is raising questions about their gender identity or sexual orientation can cause discomfort in some fathers. Fathers need to educate themselves about gender identity and sexual orientation. They may also benefit from turning to trusted family members, particularly those who identify as part of the LGBTQ community, religious leaders, or school counselors to better understand their child's evolving identity.

LGBTQ youth are often bullied by their peers; we talked about bullying in Chapter 6. Fathers should become aware of possible signs that their child is being bullied. Adolescents may become withdrawn, depressed, or anxious about going to school if they are being bullied. The Canadian Pediatric Society provides helpful suggestions about talking with one's child about gender identity (see Text Box 7.5).[48]

---

**TEXT BOX 7.5**

**Talking with Your Child about Gender Identity**

◆ Ask questions! This is a great way to hear your child's ideas about gender.

◆ Don't pressure your child to change who they are.

◆ Find opportunities to show your child that there are other gender-diverse and transgender people in your community who can appreciate them.

Source: Canadian Pediatric Society (n.d.), *Gender identity*.

---

## Cognitive Development

The major development in cognition during adolescence is the emergence of abstract thinking. There are many aspects of abstract thinking, which tends to develop gradually over the course of adolescence. Adolescents are now able to understand complex concepts such as democracy, society, religion, and politics.[49] Their knowledge of science increases in large part because they develop an understanding of abstract concepts. For example, biology is taught during high school rather than during the earlier school years because children can better understand abstract biological concepts, such as the idea that death occurs when the organs of the body stop functioning. They are better able to ask questions and analyze situations, think critically about relationships with others, think about how to influence relationships, and consider future goals.

Fathers do many things to stimulate children's cognitive skills during childhood. They read to their children, visit museums or science centers, play board games, and engage in math games. Parents' engagement in cognitive stimulation tends to decline during adolescence.[50] The Cincinnati Children's Hospital provides some helpful ideas for fathers to enhance adolescent cognitive abilities (see Text Box 7.6).[51]

## Social Development

Adolescents' desire for more independence and autonomy coincides with their desire to spend more time with peers. Adolescents desire to have more control over their lives and greater freedom to make their own decisions.

**Friendships and Peer Influence.** Parents tend to give their adolescents more freedom to make their own decisions about who their friends are and how they spend time with them.

---

TEXT BOX 7.6

**How Fathers Can Enhance Adolescents' Cognitive Abilities**

◆ Help adolescents get adequate sleep, hydration, and nutrition
◆ Include adolescents in discussions about a variety of topics, issues, and current events
◆ Encourage adolescents to share ideas and thoughts with adults
◆ Encourage adolescents to think independently and develop their own ideas
◆ Help adolescents set their own goals
◆ Encourage adolescents to think about possibilities of the future
◆ Compliment and praise adolescents for well-thought-out decisions
◆ Help adolescents to review any poorly made decisions
    Source: Cincinnati Children's Hospital (n.d.), *What is cognitive development?*

---

The creation of close friendships is one of the most important developmental tasks of adolescence. Friends provide teens with a sense of belonging and contribute greatly to their well-being and self-esteem. They are also an important source of support. Friends may help teens to get through difficult times. They provide support to adolescents who are exploring identity issues such as race/ethnicity, gender, or sexual orientation. Peers are also important agents of socialization. They provide adolescents with opportunities to develop new social skills, meet different types of people, and have new experiences. Peers set standards for positive social behaviors, such as cooperating with the group. Adolescents may belong to one or two peer groups that regularly socialize together.

Peers can also have a negative influence on adolescents. Some teens are very susceptible to peer pressure. These teens may go along with the group even though they do not think they should. Adolescents may believe that the costs associated with noncompliance with the group are too great, including being shunned or criticized by group members. Other teens encourage their friends to engage in risky activities. The peer group can embolden teens to risk shoplifting or experimenting with drugs. Fathers play an important role in preventing risky youth behavior. In a study of 287 Black female adolescents, youth expressed fewer intentions to engage in risky behaviors when they felt close to their biological fathers and when their fathers engaged in activities with them.[52] Youth are also significantly less likely to engage in delinquent behavior and substance use when they have positive, warm relationships with their fathers and when fathers are less authoritarian.[53]

**Parental Monitoring.** Parental monitoring becomes very important during adolescence. Parental monitoring is defined as parents' knowledge about their children's activities, who they hang out with, and what they do.[54] This includes monitoring social media use (we delve more into this topic later in this chapter). Close and supportive parental monitoring is an important protective factor for adolescents and can significantly reduce the chances that children will engage in delinquent and risky behaviors.[55] We emphasize here that parental monitoring should be conducted in a respectful manner. Adolescents can become extremely upset if their fathers embarrass them in the presence of peers. Fathers should listen to their adolescents without judgment and reaction. Fathers will get to know a great deal about their child's activities and behaviors when they actively listen to them. Jay recalls spending many Saturday afternoons listening to his daughters and their friends while driving them to their

activities. He learned a lot about their activities and friendships and felt more comfortable with his daughters' striving for
independence.

## Challenging Issues during Adolescence

Adolescence presents many potential challenges for fathers.
Teens frequently start drinking alcohol and using drugs. They
may engage in delinquent behaviors such as shoplifting or cutting school. They may become overly involved in internet gam-
ing or social media use. We address alcohol and drug use and
social media involvement here.

**Alcohol and Drug Use.** Alcohol is the most commonly used
substance in the United States. The National Center for Drug
Abuse Statistics reported in 2020 that 9.15% of youth ages 12 to
17 drank alcohol in the previous month.[56] Alcohol use increases
in frequency and amount as teens get older. For example, 16.8%
of 12th graders had five or more drinks in a row when consum-
ing alcohol. About 8.33% of 12- to 17-year-olds surveyed in 2020
reported using drugs (mostly marijuana) in the previous month.

Adolescents often do not see the potential dangers of using
substances, but the adolescent brain is particularly vulnerable to
the negative effects of alcohol.[57] Adolescents who start to drink
before the age of 15 years are four times more likely to meet criteria for alcohol dependence in later years. Adolescents who use
substances are also more likely to miss school, engage in sexual
risk taking, and engage in physical fighting with peers.[58]

Fathers vary greatly in their attitudes about alcohol and drug
use. Some fathers believe that their children should not engage in
alcohol or drug use at all, or not until they are adults or at least
leave home (such as for college). Other fathers are accepting of
some alcohol and drug use as long as the teen does not over-use
substances and does not engage in other risky behaviors such as
driving under the influence. Some fathers are themselves regular
users of alcohol and drugs and do not feel that they can place
restrictions on their teen's use of these substances because they
themselves are users. Fathers may serve as models (good or bad)

for adolescent substance use. Interestingly, research has shown that girls and boys modeled their father's alcohol use if they had a relatively good or moderate relationship with the father.[59] They did not model their father's alcohol use if the relationship with that parent was relatively poor. Fathers who want their children to abstain from alcohol use may find that their efforts to restrict adolescents' drinking are ineffective if they themselves are regular users.

We wrote earlier in this chapter that parental monitoring is an important protective factor for adolescents and can significantly reduce delinquent and risky behaviors. Parental monitoring is also important for protecting youth from using and abusing substances. Adolescents are significantly less likely to use substances when fathers monitor their teens' substance use.[60] Fathers should talk openly with their youth about substance use. Some teens do not want to use substances but do so because of peer pressure. Fathers can help their teen to come up with answers that they feel comfortable with when peers pressure them to drink or use drugs. Fathers can also ask their adolescents their views about drinking, getting drunk, or using substances. Opioid use and addiction have become an epidemic in the United States and in other parts of the world. Fathers should ask their children what they understand about the risks of opioid use. They should also ask their teens what they understand about drugs that are laced with fentanyl, a substance that is highly toxic and has caused many deaths in recent years.

**Social Media Use.** A 2010 study by the Kaiser Family Foundation found that American adolescents use social media more than seven hours per day, on average. Studies show both negative and positive effects of social media use on youth. Negative effects of *high levels* of social media use include communicating less with family members, lower school performance, less time spent in extracurricular activities and hobbies, and increased risk for obesity, loneliness, and depression.[61] A large-scale study conducted in the United States reported that teens often feel overwhelmed by "drama" in social media, they feel their friends are "leaving them out of things," and they feel pressure to post content that will get lots of comments or likes.[62] Several studies have painted a grim picture of the risks of excessive social media use. Economist Jonathan Rothwell found that teens who spend more than five hours a day on social media were 60% more likely to express suicidal thoughts or harm themselves, 2.8 times more likely to hold a negative view of their body, and 30% more likely to report a lot of sadness the day before.[63] However, teens tend to report more positive than negative experiences from social media use. They report feeling more connected to their friends, they like having a place to show their creative side, and they like having people who can support them through tough times.[64]

Fathers can talk with their teens about the inability of anyone to control words and images once they are posted or shared on the internet. Some adolescents and adults have lost opportunities for education or jobs, or have had their reputations negatively affected, because of ill-advised words or images they posted as teens. Sexting, or sending nude or sexually explicit pictures of oneself through the internet, is another trap for teens. It is impossible to control what happens to those images, even if they are sent to a person the adolescent thinks they can trust. Further, bad actors have requested such images from adolescents and then used them to blackmail teens or used artificial intelligence to create more explicit images of the teen and post them on porn sites, where they are almost impossible to remove. Fathers can warn their teens about the never-ending nature of words and images posted on social media and the internet, and help them take a long-term view when posting and sharing.

Social media can be used to strengthen family ties. Interviews with adolescents and their parents indicate that social media use can be a form of family entertainment and spending time together, a resource for information, a means for making emotional connections in the family (such as sharing photos together), and a means for documenting family events and experiences.[65]

The research on social media use among adolescents can be confusing for fathers when both positive and negative effects are reported. Clearly, social media use can have negative effects on youth and drive a wedge in family relationships. Fathers may tend to view social media use through a negative lens, but they should also acknowledge the positives. The American Academy of Pediatrics (AAP) recommends that families create a family media plan with their adolescents.[66] The AAP provides a template on the internet for families to develop this plan, which includes recommendations for screen time, choosing good content, communicating about media, and families using media together. For example, the AAP recommends that parents create areas in their home that are screen-free. The AAP also recommends that parents talk with children about time limits and explain why it is important to develop self-control by turning off screens.

## Summary

Raising adolescent children can be challenging and joyful at the same time. Fathers' attitudes matter a great deal. Fathers who have positive attitudes about their child's increasing desire for independence are likely to enjoy watching their child grow up. They will not be bothered when adolescents make mistakes or sometimes fall short of following family rules. They can enjoy the many positives of raising adolescents: watching their child become more like an adult, having adult conversations with the child, and realizing that their child is socially aware and has opinions about important topics (e.g., politics). Raising an adolescent can also be a source of considerable anxiety for fathers. Adolescents may engage in risky behaviors, they may become rebellious, and they may make poor decisions that can have long-lasting effects on themselves and their parents. Fathers who have concerns about their child's behavior can benefit from and should reach out for support from other parents, friends, relatives, and professionals such as family therapists, psychologists, and social workers.

## Notes

1 Paris, J., Ricardo, A., & Rymond, D. (2019). *Child growth and development*. College of the Canyons.
2 Phares, V., Fields, S., & Kamboukos, D. (2009). Fathers' and mothers' involvement with their adolescents. *Journal of Child and Family Studies, 18*, 1–9. https://doi.org/10.1007/s10826-008-9200-7

3 Kobak, R., Abbott, C., Zisk, A., & Bounoua, N. (2017). Adapting to the changing needs of adolescents: Parenting practices and challenges to sensitive attunement. *Current Opinions in Psychology, 15,* 137–142. https://doi.org /10.1016/j.copsyc.2017.02.018

4 Kobak, R., Abbott, C., Zisk, A., & Bounoua, N. (2017). Adapting to the changing needs of adolescents.

5 Zarrett, N., & Eccles, J. (2006). The passage to adulthood: Challenges of late adolescence. *New Directions for Youth Development, 111,* 13–27. https://doi .org/10.1002/yd.179

6 Smetana, J. G., & Asquith, P. (1994). Adolescents' and parents' conceptions of parental authority and personal autonomy. *Child Development, 65*(4), 1147–1162. https://doi.org/10.1111/j.1467-8624.1994.tb00809.x

7 Shearer, C. L., Crouter, A. C., & McHale, S. M. (2005). Parents' perceptions of changes in mother–child and father–child relationships during adolescence. *Journal of Adolescent Research, 20*(6), 662–684. https://doi.org/10.1177 /0743558405275086

8 Stewart, J. L., Widman, L., & Kamke, K. (2019). Applying a multifactorial communication framework to better understand differences between father–daughter and mother–daughter sexual health discussions. *Journal of Health Communication, 24*(7–8), 633–642. https://doi-org.libproxy.temple.edu /10.1080/10810730.2019.1651428

9 Stewart, J. L., Widman, L., & Kamke, K. (2019). Applying a multifactorial communication framework.

10 Blickman, R. S., & Campbell, C. G. (2022). Moving toward an integrated model of the father–daughter relationship during adolescence. *Family Relations, 72,* 2664–2678. https://doi.org/10.1111/fare.12787

11 Dunleavy, K. N., Wanzer, M. B., Krezmien, E., & Ruppel, K. (2011). Daughters' perceptions of communication with their fathers: The role of skill similarity and co-orientation in relationship satisfaction. *Communication Studies, 62*(5), 581–596. https://doi.org/10.1080/10510974.2011.588983

12 O'Gara, J. L., Zhang, A., Padilla, Y., Liu, C., & Wang, K. (2019). Father–youth closeness and adolescent self-rated health: The mediating role of mental health. *Children and Youth Services Review, 104,* 104386. https://doi.org/10 .1016/j.childyouth.2019.104386

13 Roubinov, D. S., & Boyce, W. T. (2017). Parenting and SES: Relative values or enduring principles? *Current Opinion in Psychology, 15,* 162–167. https://doi .org/10.1016/j.copsyc.2017.03.001

14 Weissbourd, R., Batanova, M., Laski, M., McIntyre, J., Torres, E., & Balisciano, N. (2023). *Caring for the caregivers: The critical link between parent and teen mental health.* https://mcc.gse.harvard.edu/reports/caring-for-the-caregiver

15 Kobak, R., Abbott, C., Zisk, A., & Bounoua, N. (2017). Adapting to the changing needs of adolescents.

16 Teubert, D., & Pinquart, M. (2011). The link between coparenting, parenting, and adolescent life satisfaction. *Family Science, 2*(4), 221–229. https://doi .org/10.1080/19424620.2012.666655

17 Feinberg, M. E., Kan, M. L., & Hetherington, E. M. (2007). The longitudinal influence of coparenting conflict on parental negativity and adolescent maladjustment. *Journal of Marriage and Family, 69,* 687–702. https://doi.org /10.1111/j.1741-3737.2007.00400.x

18 Teubert, D., & Pinquart, M. (2011). The link between coparenting, parenting, and adolescent life satisfaction.

19 Feinberg, M. E., Kan, M. L., & Hetherington, E. M. (2007). The longitudinal influence of coparenting conflict.

20  Paris, J., Ricardo, A., & Rymond, D. (2019). *Child growth and development.*
21  Mendle, J., Turkheimer, E., & Emery, R. E. (2007). Detrimental psychological outcomes associated with early pubertal timing in adolescent girls. *Developmental Review, 27*(2), 151–171. https://doi.org/10.1016/j.dr.2006.11.001
22  Klopack, E. T., Sutton, T. E., Simons, R. L., & Simons, L. G. (2020). Disentangling the effects of boys' pubertal timing: The importance of social context. *Journal of Youth and Adolescence, 49*(7), 1393–1405. https://doi.org/10.1007/s10964-019-01141-9
23  Draper, P., & Harpending, H. (1982). Father absence and reproductive strategy: An evolutionary perspective. *Journal of Anthropological Research, 38,* 255–273. https://doi.org/10.1086/jar.38.3.3629848
24  Webster, G. D., Graber, J. A., Gesselman, A. N., Crosier, B. S., & Schember, T. O. (2014). A life history theory of father absence and menarche: A meta-analysis. *Evolutionary Psychology, 12*(2), 273–294. https://doi.org/10.1177/147470491401200202
25  Sear, R., Sheppard, P., & Coall, D. A. (2019). Cross-cultural evidence does not support universal acceleration of puberty in father-absent households. *Philosophical Transactions of the Royal Society B, 374,* 20180124. http://doi.org/10.1098/rstb.2018.0124
26  Ogletree, M. D., Jones, R. M., & Coyl, D. D. (2002). Fathers and their adolescent sons: Pubertal development and paternal involvement. *Journal of Adolescent Research, 17*(4), 418–424. https://doi.org/10.1177/07458402017004006
27  Brooks-Gunn, J., & Zahaykevich, M. (1989). Parent–daughter relationships in early adolescence. In K. Kreppner & R. M. Lerner (Eds.), *Family systems and life-span development* (pp. 223–246). Lawrence Erlbaum Associates.
28  Paris, J., Ricardo, A., & Rymond, D. (2019). *Child growth and development.*
29  Paruthi, S., Brooks, L. J., D'Ambrosio, C., Hall, W. A., Kotagal, S., Lloyd, R. M., Malow, B. A., Maski, K., Nichols, C., Quan, S. F., Rosen, C. L., Troester, M. M., & Wise, M. S. (2016). Consensus statement of the American Academy of Sleep Medicine on the recommended amount of sleep for healthy children: Methodology and discussion. *Journal of Clinical Sleep Medicine, 12,* 1549–1561. https://doi.org/10.5664/jcsm.6288
30  Centers for Disease Control and Prevention. (n.d.). *Sleep in middle and high school students.* www.cdc.gov/healthyschools/features/students-sleep .htm#:~:text=Importance%20of%20Sleep&text=The%20American%20Aca demy%20of%20Sleep,10%20hours%20per%2024%20hours
31  Mullan, K. (2019). A child's day: Trends in time use in the UK from 1975 to 2015. *British Journal of Sociology, 70,* 997–1024. https://doi-org.libproxy.temple.edu/10.1111/1468-4446.12369
32  Abma, J. C., & Martinez, G. M. (2017). *Sexual activity and contraceptive use among teenagers in the United States, 2011–2015.* https://www.cdc.gov/nchs/data/nhsr/nhsr104.pdf
33  Scull, T. M., Carl, A. E., Keefe, E. M., & Malik, C. V. (2022). Exploring parent-gender differences in parent and adolescent reports of the frequency, quality, and content of their sexual health communication. *The Journal of Sex Research, 59*(1), 122–134. https://doi.org/10.1080/00224499.2021.1936439
34  Centers for Disease Control and Prevention. (n.d.). *Talking with your teen about sex.* www.cdc.gov/healthyyouth/protective/factsheets/talking_teens .htm
35  Wilson, R. L., & Wilson, R. (2014). *Understanding emotional development.* Routledge.
36  von Tetzchner, S. (2022). Emotional development in childhood and adolescence. In S. von Tetzchner (Ed.), *Typical and atypical child and adolescent*

*development: Emotions, temperament, personality, moral, prosocial and antisocial development.* Routledge.

37 American Psychological Association. (n.d.). *Identity.* https://dictionary.apa .org/Identity

38 Scheuringer, B. (2016). Multiple identities: A theoretical and an empirical approach. *European Review, 24*(3), 397–404. https://doi.org/10.1017/ S1062798716000120

39 Crocetti, E., Albarello, F., Meeus, W., & Rubini, M. (2023). Identities: A developmental social–psychological perspective. *European Review of Social Psychology, 34*(1), 161–201. https://doi.org/10.1080/10463283.2022.2104987

40 Beyers, W., & Goossens, L. (2008). Dynamics of perceived parenting and identity formation in late adolescence. *Journal of Adolescence, 31*(2), 165–184. https://doi.org/10.1016/j.adolescence.2007.04.003

41 Beyers, W., & Goossens, L. (2008). Dynamics of perceived parenting and identity formation in late adolescence.

42 Brittian, A. S. (2012). Understanding African American adolescents' identity development: A relational developmental systems perspective. *Journal of Black Psychology, 38*(2), 172–200. https://doi.org/10.1177/0095798411414570

43 Stevenson, H. C. (1994). Validation of the Scale of Racial Socialization for African American adolescents: Steps toward multidimensionality. *Journal of Black Psychology, 20*(4), 445–468. https://doi.org/10.1177/00957984940204005

44 Boykin, A. W., & Toms, F. D. (1985). Black child socialization: A conceptual framework. In H. P. McAdoo & J. L. McAdoo (Eds.), *Black children: Social, educational, and parental environments* (pp. 33–51). Sage Publications; see also Belgrave, F. Z., & Brevard, J. K. (2015). *African American boys' identity, culture, and development.* Springer.

45 American Psychological Association. (n.d.). *Identity.* https://dictionary.apa .org/Identity

46 American Psychological Association. (n.d.). *Identity.* https://dictionary.apa .org/Identity

47 de Vries, A. L., Kreukels, B. P., Steensma, T. D., & McGuire, J. K. (2014). Gender identity development: A biopsychosocial perspective. In *Gender dysphoria and disorders of sex development: Progress in care and knowledge* (pp. 53–80) (Focus on Sexuality Research). Springer.

48 Canadian Pediatric Society. (n.d.). *Gender identity.* https://caringforkids.cps .ca/handouts/behavior-and-development/gender-identity

49 Lehalle, H. (2019). Cognitive development in adolescence: Thinking freed from concrete constraints. In S. Jackson & L. Goosens (Eds.), *Handbook of adolescent development.* Psychology Press. https://doi.org/10.4324 /9780203969861

50 Simpkins, S. D., Bouffard, S. M., Dearing, E., Kreider, H., Wimer, C., Caronongan, P., & Weiss, H. B. (2009). Adolescent adjustment and patterns of parents' behaviors in early and middle adolescence. *Journal of Research on Adolescence, 19*(3), 530–557. https://doi.org/10.1111/J.1532-7795.2009.00606.X

51 Cincinnati Children's. (n.d.). *What is cognitive development.* www.cincinnati-childrens.org/health/c/cognitive-development

52 Cryer-Coupet, Q. R., Dorsey, M. S., Lemmons, B., & Hope, E. C. (2020). Examining multiple dimensions of father involvement as predictors of risk-taking intentions among Black adolescent females. *Children and Youth Services Review, 108,* 104604. https://doi.org/10.1016/j.childyouth.2019 .104604

53 Bronte-Tinkew, J., Moore, K. A., & Carrano, J. (2006). The father–child relationship, parenting styles, and adolescent risk behaviors in intact

families. *Journal of Family Issues*, *27*(6), 850–881. https://doi.org/10.1177/0192513X05285296

54  Paris, J., Ricardo, A., & Rymond, D. (2019). *Child growth and development.*

55  Hoeve, M., Dubas, J. S., Eichelsheim, V. I., van der Laan, P. H., Smeenk, W., & Gerris, J. R. (2009). The relationship between parenting and delinquency: A meta-analysis. *Journal of Abnormal Child Psychology*, *37*, 749–775. https://doi.org/10.1007/s10802-009-9310-8

56  National Center for Drug Abuse Statistics. (2020). *Drug use among youth: Facts & statistics.* drugabusestatistics.org/teen-drug use/#:~:text=Alcohol%20is%20by%20far%20the,drinking%20in%20the%20last%20month

57  Welch, K. A., Carson, A., & Lawrie, S. M. (2013). Brain structure in adolescents and young adults with alcohol problems: Systematic review of imaging studies. *Alcohol*, *48*, 433–444. https://doi.org/10.1093/alcalc/agt037

58  Parsai, M., Voisine, S., Marsiglia, F. F., Kulis, S., & Nieri, T. (2009). The protective and risk effects of parents and peers on substance use, attitudes and behaviors of Mexican and Mexican American female and male adolescents. *Youth and Society*, *40*(3), 353–376. https://doi.org/10.1177/0044118X08318117

59  Andrews, J. A., Hops, H., & Duncan, S. C. (1997). Adolescent modeling of parent substance use: The moderating effect of the relationship with the parent. *Journal of Family Psychology*, *11*(3), 259–270. https://doi.org/10.1037/0893-3200.11.3.259

60  Luk, J. W., King, K. M., McCarty, C. A., McCauley, E., & Stoep, A. (2017). Prospective effects of parenting on substance use and problems across Asian/Pacific Islander and European American youth: Tests of moderated mediation. *Journal of Studies in Alcohol and Drugs*, *78*(4), 521–530. https://doi.org/10.15288/jsad.2017.78.521

61  Coyne, S. M., Padilla-Walker, L. M., Fraser, A. M., Fellows, K., & Day, R. D. (2014). "Media time = family time": Positive media use in families with adolescents. *Journal of Adolescent Research*, *29*(5), 663–688. https://doi.org/10.1177/0743558414538316

62  Vogels, E. A., & Gelles-Watnick, R. (2023). *Teens and social media: Key findings from Pew Research Center surveys.* www.pewresearch.org/short-reads/2023/04/24/teens-and-social-media-key-findings-from-pew-research-center-surveys/#:~:text=Some%20teens%20report%20using%20these,to%20give%20up%20social%20media

63  Rothwell, J. (2023). *How parenting and self-control mediate the link between social media use and youth mental health.* Institute for Family Studies. https://ifstudies.org/blog/how-parenting-and-self-control-mediate-the-link-between-social-media-use-and-youth-mental-health

64  Vogels, E. A., & Gelles-Watnick, R. (2023). Teens and social media.

65  Coyne, S. M., Padilla-Walker, L. M., Fraser, A. M., Fellows, K., & Day, R. D. (2014). "Media time = family time".

66  American Academy of Pediatrics. (n.d.). *The family media plan.* https://www.healthychildren.org/English/fmp/Pages/MediaPlan.aspx

# 8

# Fathers and Young Adults

## Letting Go and Providing a Secure Base as Needed

*The most exciting thing is seeing what these kids are developing into. Two are out of college and one is in college. They are just finding their own way as individuals. … This past couple months has been particularly exciting for me as a dad because all three girls are doing their own thing in different fields, and here's my stepson doing his own thing, but still influenced by me and his mom. … My daughter has this traveling spirit, and she is now in [California] working as a traveling nurse. The joy for me as a dad is she related it to when I was 24 and I went to California [to work]. I was so proud of her that she decided to travel across country and become a travel nurse and to weave in, "kind of like you did dad when you graduated college and went to California to start your career … ." It's enough to make you cry. … As a dad I am seeing these kids go for it and do the things they think they are passionate about, but it could change … . For me, the joy comes in all of these kids as they are coming into their own in young adulthood. … It makes you feel like you did something right. … Now they are young adults, you can talk more freely about family issues and treat them as adults and not kids, which I am used to treating them as kids, and I have to let that go.*

*[The challenge is] the worry. You have a kid driving across country. … I send them safety tips that come across Instagram. … how to get into your car at night in a parking lot. If someone pulls you over, do this, don't do that. I'd rather they make fun of me for that than not having sent it. For me the challenge is the worry.*

—*Divorced father of three daughters, ages 20, 22, and 24,*
*and stepfather of a son, age 18*

## Introduction

The focus in the book up to this point has been on fathers and children from before birth to adolescence. It is probably safe to say that fathers and mothers have their greatest impact on children in those stages of development. But parenting does not stop once children reach adulthood. Fathers continue to be involved

DOI: 10.4324/9781003486107-8

with adult children, support them in multiple ways, and influence their growth and development. The quote from the father at the beginning of this chapter shows clearly how fathers stay involved with their adult children and influence their development. Adulthood is not a single monolithic stage in one's life. Eric Erikson's theory of biopsychosocial development suggests that development does not end during childhood, but continues into adulthood.[1]

Adulthood is made up of three major stages of development. Young adulthood goes from ages 20 to 40 and is the period when individuals make important life decisions about occupation, social roles, intimate relationships, and parenthood. Middle adulthood goes from ages 41 to 64 and is the stage when many adults are intensely involved in caring for and raising children. Middle-aged adults tend to be at the peak of their careers. Older adulthood starts at age 65 and is the stage when many adults wind down their careers, help with grandchildren, and become involved in activities that they find meaningful, such as volunteer work. Older adults may experience an increasing number of health problems and rely on their adult children for help in daily activities, such as driving and self-care.

This chapter focuses on fathers and young adults between the ages of 18 and 25. Jeffrey Arnett has labeled this period of development *emerging adulthood*.[2] This stage is characterized by identity exploration, including exploration of world views, work roles, friendships, and intimate relationships. Emerging adults often feel they are in between adolescence and adulthood. It is also a period of instability related to work, residence, education, and relationships. Arnett describes emerging adults as being very self-focused, that is, they are concerned primarily with themselves, including their own desires and needs.[3] Many young adults experience a great deal of personal growth between ages 18 and 25 in education, employment, interpersonal relationships, and sometimes parenthood. We focus on emerging adulthood because young adults may still rely on their parents to a greater extent during this stage of adulthood than in later periods of adult development. We use the terms *emerging adults, young adults,* and *emerging adult children* interchangeably throughout this chapter.

In this chapter, we discuss the developmental characteristics and tasks of young adults and focus less on the specific developmental domains that were addressed in other chapters. We also examine the developmental tasks and challenges of fathers during this stage while considering the social, economic, and cultural contexts. The final section of the chapter addresses nonresident fathers and their relationships with emerging adults.

## Emerging Adult Developmental Tasks

During emerging adulthood, young adults undergo a shift from being dependent on fathers and mothers to being more independent. Their status as adults is marked by legal rights in the United States, such as being able to vote and enlist in the military at age 18 and being able to purchase and drink alcohol at age 21. Most young adults start to work, and some continue postsecondary education and even earn advanced degrees. Emerging adults are also likely to form close intimate relationships. However, their commitment to roles and relationships tend to be temporary. They may apply to a graduate program only to decide that the program does not fulfill their career goals. They may explore career options through unpaid internships. They may embark on a career only to find that it does not suit them. Young adults may go from one romantic relationship to another, trying to discover what type of partner is a good fit with them. Most young adults do not marry until their late 20s and many young adults live together before or instead of marriage.[4]

Neuroscience research has begun to focus on brain development during emerging adulthood.[5] The brain's prefrontal cortex continues to change during ages 18 to 25, which leads to improvement in executive function.[6] Young adults are able to make better decisions, plan ahead, solve problems, and evaluate risk and reward; their ability to use good judgment improves. There is also improved communication between the frontal cortex and areas of the brain associated with emotions and impulses. This can lead to better self-control and improved regulation of emotions. Emerging adulthood is also a period when many young adults undergo personality changes. For example, they may become more sociable, whereas they tended to be cautious in personal relationships when they were younger. They are also vulnerable to taking more risks as they gain more freedom from parental supervision.

Larry Nelson and his colleagues conducted a study about the criteria parents and emerging adults consider necessary to achieving adulthood.[7] The young adults in the study were unmarried college students. Fathers, mothers, and emerging adults selected four characteristics that they considered necessary to being an adult. The four that emerging adults identified were: (1) accept responsibility and the consequences for your actions, (2) establish relationships with parents as equals, (3) become financially independent from parents, and (4) decide on beliefs/values independently of parents. For fathers, the top items were: (1) accept responsibility and the consequences of your own actions, (2) avoid committing petty crimes and vandalism, (3) avoid drunk driving, and (4) become less self-oriented and develop greater consideration for others. Both fathers and emerging adult children were concerned with relational maturity. Fathers expressed more concern over compliance with norms, while emerging adults were more concerned with independence. Fathers' concerns are perhaps warranted, given the number of emerging adults who are arrested and incarcerated (29%) versus the percent of the population they represent (10%).[8]

We have emphasized in this book that context matters. This is very much the case for emerging adults. One shifting social context is the changing attitudes and behaviors around cohabitation and marriage. Cohabitation has become the dominant form of first union and is less stable than marriage.[9] Another shifting social context is the economy—economic changes have made living independently more challenging for young adults and currently 52% of emerging adults live with their parents.[10] The rising cost of postsecondary education is another economic factor that may limit choices for some emerging adults.

Studies have suggested that emerging adulthood is a prolonged phase of development that is more likely to occur among middle-class populations. Some researchers question the extent to which emerging adulthood as a developmental stage applies to working-class youth. For example, Nancy Galambos and M. Loreto Martinez found that emerging adulthood is a privilege experienced only by middle-class young adults in Latin American countries.[11] Jeffrey Arnett examined this question in a national survey of 18- to 25-year-olds in the United States.[12] He found more consistencies than inconsistencies across social class groups in terms of three important aspects of emerging adulthood: positive and negative perceptions of the time period; views of education and work; and views of love, sex, and marriage. We expect that this debate will continue among researchers, but our experience tells us that many fathers experience their children's ups and downs during this stage of development. Social class and the related capacity for parents' financial and other support can provide more time to explore options for some emerging adults more than others.

## Developmental Tasks for Fathers of Emerging Adults

Traditionally, parents have felt relief from the responsibilities of child-rearing once a child reaches age 18. We don't necessarily think about a child's emerging adulthood as a time for fathers and mothers to continue their own parental growth, but they do. Ellen Galinsky, in her study of parents in the late 1970s, labeled this the *departure stage* and saw it as a time for parents to adapt to the child's departure with hopes that their grown child will be "settled" after being successfully launched into adulthood.[13] Because emerging adulthood can be a period of instability and vulnerability for young adults, fathers can be an important influence on their children by offering support and guidance.[14]

There are important developmental tasks for fathers of emerging adults. Fathers who are aware of emerging adults' developmental tasks and challenges can better understand young adult behavior and know how to provide support. A father's role is to continue encouraging exploration and independence, which fathers may do in several ways: providing financial support for postsecondary education, using social connections to help with finding jobs, and providing emotional support for career and family decisions. Glen remembers his own father cosigning a car loan for him; Glen did the same for his daughter 30 years later. Fathers can also be available as a safe haven, which might mean literally providing a place to live during this time or might mean being an emotional safe haven, or both. Finally, fathers can help their emerging adult children by being available as a guide or comfort during the ups and particularly the downs, such as failed romantic relationships or lost jobs.

## Ties between Young Adult Children and Fathers

The influence that fathers have on their emerging adults may be more important today than it was in earlier times because of the close ties that parents have with their children. In 2001, Vern Bengston wrote a paper suggesting that ties between parents and adult children would become increasingly important in the twenty-first century.[15] Bengston argued that changes in family structures and increasing longevity would result in stronger ties between parents and their adult children. Bengston's predictions appear to be supported by research. Karen Fingerman and her colleagues have suggested that the ties between parents and emerging adults in their early 20s are now more important than any other adult relationships.[16] A number of factors contribute to the increasing importance of ties between parents and young adults. Later ages of first marriage mean than many young adults are not in stable, long-term romantic relationships, so they rely more on their parents for emotional support. The Great Recession of 2007–2008 also contributed to young adults having stronger ties with parents because they were less likely to be able to complete their education, find well-paying jobs, and establish careers. The rising costs of higher education compelled many young adults to incur large student loans.[17] Many young adults were forced to live with their parents because they could not afford to live on their own. The trend for young adults to live with parents has continued through the early 2020s. The Covid-19 pandemic brought many young adults back into their parents' homes. Rather than live alone or with roommates at a time when there were restrictions on social life, many young adults returned home or never left their parents' homes.[18] Technological advances have also contributed to stronger ties between parents and young adults. Cell phones, email, text messages, and other technologies have made communication between young adults and their parents more frequent and less costly.[19]

Ties between fathers and their emerging adult children may be influenced when young adults have their own children during the late teens or early 20s. Although many young adults delay childbearing until their late 20s or 30s, some have children earlier. The birth of children often brings fathers and their adult children closer together. New parents may turn to their fathers and mothers for advice and support. Fathers may enjoy the opportunity to mentor their son or daughter through the experience of caring for a newborn. Fathers often welcome the opportunity to become a grandfather and experience great joy in this new role. There are also challenges with becoming a grandfather when a son or daughter is still in their teens or early 20s. Fathers may still be raising younger children who live at home and may experience disappointment if their young adult does not finish school or cannot financially support the child.

Having closer ties with fathers today than in past generations does not necessarily mean that young adults have better relationships with fathers. Attachment to fathers tends to decline as young adults grow older[20] or when they are in romantic relationships. Many young adults and their fathers report tension in their relationships—one of them is bothered by some issue in the relationship, even if they don't talk about it. In a study of young adult children (most of whom were married) and their parents, nearly all fathers and children reported at least a small amount of tension in their relationship.[21] Both fathers and mothers reported more intense tension than their young adult offspring, especially over issues such as finances and education. These tensions may reflect parents' worries and irritations regarding their children's lack of progress in becoming self-sufficient adults.[22] Young adults tend to feel more relationship tension from mothers than fathers.

An example of relationship tension for young adults is a feeling that their parents are intruding on their privacy.

## Young Adults Who Live with Their Parents

Conflict between fathers and young adults can be exacerbated when young adults reside with parents. Fathers have more opportunities to observe and experience their young adult's behavior when they reside in the same household. Young adults may have lived apart from their parents during or after college, and upon returning home, expect to be treated as if they are still to be cared for as dependents rather than independent, responsible adults. They may be unwilling to clean up after themselves, stay up late with friends in the house, or not contribute to household chores or meal preparation. Fathers, mothers, and their adult children benefit from having a frank conversation about reasonable expectations of one another before the young adult moves back home. For example, making it clear how household chores and cooking will be shared, whether the young adult will pay rent or help pay for groceries and utilities, what the house rules for guests are, and how everyone's privacy will be respected can help to reduce potential relationship conflict. Family members may find it helpful to write a contract that reflects everyone's expectations.

## Expectations between Young Adult Children and Fathers

Emerging adults and their fathers can run into problems when their expectations for each other don't match up. Some young adult children seem to lack motivation to grow up. They struggle with completing their education or obtaining paid work. Some young adults need more time than their peers (or than their parents did) to find a direction in life. They may be reluctant to finish their post-secondary education if they are uncertain about their career. Conflict may occur when fathers pressure their children to make better decisions or do more with their lives. Conversely, fathers may have a difficult time letting go or feel they need to rescue their young adult children. Adult children may also have unrealistic expectations of their fathers. They may expect their fathers to support or house them when they are not willing or able to obtain paid work. Or they may believe their fathers want to be too involved in their lives or decisions.

Unrealistic expectations can drive fathers and their children apart. They can cause frustration, anxiety, disappointment, low self-esteem, and anger. These emotional reactions sometimes result in fathers or children withdrawing from the relationship, engaging in intense conflict, or suffering increased health and mental health problems.

Fathers and children should strive to have reasonable expectations of one another. They should have open communication and treat each other with kindness, honesty, and respect. Fathers should think of ways to be supportive rather than judgmental of their young adult children. Being supportive may mean simply listening to a child and finding out how they are doing. Young adult children who are struggling to find a direction in their lives often benefit from seeing a mental health professional. Fathers should encourage their children to see a therapist if they are having a hard time.

## Challenges for Fathers with Young Adult Children

Fathers may face a number of challenges as they try to support their emerging adult children. Substance abuse is at its peak during young adulthood, with 24% of adults ages 18–25 having used an illicit drug during the last 30 days.[23] According to the American Addictions Centers, alcohol abuse also peaks during this time, with 1 in 11 young adults being a heavy drinker.[24] Mental health issues are often related to substance abuse, but they may be unrelated to substance abuse. One third of emerging adults faced a mental health issue and 11.4% had a serious mental health issue in 2023.[25]

Nonmarital childbearing is another common challenge, with two thirds of births to women ages 20–24 occurring outside marriage.[26] Just when fathers and mothers expect relief from the responsibilities of child-rearing when a child reaches young adulthood, the birth of grandchildren outside marriage or in a cohabiting relationship can put the new grandparents in the position of having to help care for young children. Substance abuse, mental health issues, and nonmarital childbearing may interfere with emerging adults' ability to establish a career path or develop long-term intimate relationships.

As fathers encounter some of the challenges of managing their relationships with their young adult children, it can be helpful to take time to reflect. Here are a few questions to reflect on as you consider your role as a father of an emerging adult.

### Reflection Questions

- ◆ How would you describe your current relationship with your young adult child?
- ◆ What hopes do you have for your adult child?
- ◆ What expectations do you have of yourself as a father of an emerging adult?
- ◆ What areas of conflict get in the way of your relationship with your adult child?
- ◆ What strengths do you bring to your relationship with your emerging adult?

## Nonresident Fathers and Young Adults

Throughout this book, we have documented the challenges that nonresident fathers experience in staying connected to their children. These challenges persist for many nonresident fathers who did not live with their children during their childhood years as their children enter adulthood. That is not to say that all nonresident fathers and young adults have distant relationships. Some young adult children connect with their fathers to a greater extent than they did during childhood because they are more mobile (e.g., they own a car) or because their mothers exert less influence over them. Many young adults have said that their relationships with fathers improved or remained stable when they became adults.[27] All told, young adults in the United States have in-person contact with their nonresident fathers on average one to three times per month.[28]

Several factors influence young adult–nonresident father relationships. Young adults are more likely to have close ties with fathers who had joint custody of children and who had early and regular contact with children.[29] Young adults report better communication with divorced fathers when there were fewer unresolved conflicts in the father–child relationship.[30] Nonresident fathers who repartnered or remarried tend to have less contact with adult children and provide less support to them than fathers who live alone.[31]

Nonresident fathers can positively influence their young adult children's well-being if they stay involved with them. Young adults report greater intimacy, security, commitment, and trust in their own romantic relationships when nonresident fathers are highly involved with them.[32] Nonresident fathers also have an impact on young adult health. For example, higher levels of nonresidential father involvement with adolescents significantly decreased the odds of young adult cigarette smoking, especially among girls.[33]

## Summary

One of the paradoxes of a young adult's life is the desire for more independence from parents just as they are entering a long period of instability and vulnerability. This is a time when fathers' support might be essential to a successful transition to the adult roles of worker, partner, and creator of a family. In many ways the earlier model of the Circle of Security, which describes attachment relationship dynamics, comes full circle during this stage in the life of a young adult. The Circle of Security model suggests that fathers should encourage and support their children's exploration and independence. At the same time, it is also crucial for fathers to be there as a safe haven and continue to provide emotional support during the many ups and downs that young adults may encounter between ages 18 and 25.

# Notes

1 Erikson, E. (1980). *Identity and the life cycle*. W. W. Norton.
2 Arnett, J. J. (2007). Emerging adulthood: What is it and what is it good for? *Child Development Perspectives*, 1(2), 68–73.
3 Tanner, J. L., & Arnett, J. J. (2017). The emergence of emerging adulthood. In A. Furlong (Ed.), *Routledge handbook of youth and young adulthood* (2nd ed.). Routledge. https://doi-org.libproxy.temple.edu/10.4324/9781315753058
4 Brown, S. L. (2022). Union and family formation during young adulthood: Insights from Add Health. *Journal of Adolescent Health, 71*, 532–539.
5 Taber-Thomas, B., & Perez-Edgar, K. (2014). Emerging adulthood brain development. In J. Arnett (Ed.), *Oxford handbook of emerging adulthood* (pp. 1–19). Oxford University Press.
6 Simpson, A. R. (2018). *Brain changes*. MIT Young Adult Development Project. https://hr.mit.edu/static/worklife/youngadult/brain.html
7 Nelson, L. J., Padilla-Walker, L. M., Carroll, J. S., Barry, C. M., Madsen, S. D., & Badger, S. (2007). "If you want me to trust you like an adult, start acting like one!": Comparing the criteria that emerging adults and their parents have for adulthood. *Journal of Family Psychology, 21*(4), 665–674. https://doi.org/10.1037/0893-3200.21.4.665
8 National Institute of Justice. (2014). *From youth justice involvement to young adult offending*. https://nij.ojp.gov/topics/articles/youth-justice-involvement-young-adult-offending
9 Brown, S. L. (2022). Union and family formation.
10 Fry, R., Passell, J. S., & Cohn, D. (2020). *A majority of young adults in the U.S. live with their parents for the first time since the great depression*. www.pewresearch.org/short-reads/2020/09/04/a-majority-of-young-adults-in-the-u-s-live-with-their-parents-for-the-first-time-since-the-great-depression/
11 Galambos, N. L., & Martinez, M. L. (2007). Poised for emerging adulthood in Latin America: A pleasure for the privileged. *Child Development Perspectives*, 1(2), 109–114. https://doi.org/10.1111/j.1750-8606.2007.00024.x
12 Arnett, J. J. (2016). Does emerging adulthood theory apply across social classes? National data on a persistent question. *Emerging Adulthood, 4*(4), 227–235. https://doi.org/10.1177/2167696815613000
13 Galinsky, E. (1987). *The six stages of parenthood*. Addison-Wesley.
14 Soria, C., & Lawton, L. (2023). Connecting fathers: Fathers' impact on adult children's social networks. *The International Journal of Aging and Human Development, 96*(1), 19–32. https://doi.org/10.1177/00914150221106645
15 Bengtson, V. L. (2001). Beyond the nuclear family: The increasing importance of multigenerational bonds. *Journal of Marriage and Family, 63*, 1–16. https://doi.org/10.1111/j.1741-3737.2001.00001.x
16 Fingerman, K. L., Huo, M., & Birditt, K. S. (2020). A decade of research on intergenerational ties: Technological, economic, political, and demographic changes. *Journal of Marriage and Family, 82*(1), 383–403. https://doi.org/10.1111/jomf.12604
17 Padilla-Walker, L. M., Nelson, L. J., & Carroll, J. S. (2012). Affording emerging adulthood: Parental financial assistance of their college-aged children. *Journal of Adult Development, 19*, 50–58. https://doi.org/10.1007/s10804-011-9134-y
18 Fry, R., Passell, J. S., & Cohn, D. (2020). *A majority of young adults in the U.S.*
19 Fingerman, K. L., Cheng, Y. P., Tighe, L., Birditt, K. S., & Zarit, S. (2012). Relationships between young adults and their parents. In A. Booth, S.

Brown, N. Landale, W. Manning, & S. McHale (Eds.), *Early adulthood in a family context. National symposium on family issues* (Vol. 2). Springer. https://doi.org/10.1007/978-1-4614-1436-0_5

20 Freeman, H., & Almond, T. M. (2014). Mapping young adults' use of fathers for attachment support: Implications on romantic relationship experiences. In L. A. Newland, H. S. Freeman, & D. D. Coyle (Eds.), *Emerging topics on father attachment* (pp. 218–239). Routledge.

21 Birditt, K. S., Miller, L. M., Fingerman, K. L., & Lefkowitz, E. S. (2009). Tensions in the parent and adult child relationship: Links to solidarity and ambivalence. *Psychology of Aging, 24*(2), 287–295. https://doi.org/10.1037/a0015196

22 Birditt, K. S., Miller, L. M., Fingerman, K. L., & Lefkowitz, E. S. (2009). Tensions in the parent and adult child relationship.

23 SAMHSA. (2023). *Substance misuse prevention for young adults.* https://store.samhsa.gov/sites/default/files/substance-misuse-prevention-young-adults-pep19-pl-guide-1.pdf

24 American Addiction Centers. (2023, June). *Alcohol and drug abuse among young adults.* https://americanaddictioncenters.org/addiction-statistics/young-adults

25 National Institute of Mental Health. (2023, March). *Mental illness.* https://www.nimh.nih.gov/health/statistics/mental-illness#part_2539

26 Child Stats. (2023). *America's children: Key national indicators of well-being 2023.* https://www.childstats.gov/americaschildren/family2.asp

27 Ahrons, C. R., & Tanner, J. L. (2003). Adult children and their fathers: Relationship changes 20 years after parental divorce. *Family Relations, 52*(4), 340–351. https://doi.org/10.1111/j.1741-3729.2003.00340.x

28 Aquilino, W. S. (2006). The noncustodial father–child relationship from adolescence into young adulthood. *Journal of Marriage and Family, 68*(4), 929–946. https://doi.org/10.1111/j.1741-3737.2006.00305.x

29 Peters, B., & Ehrenberg, M. F. (2008). The influence of parental separation and divorce on father–child relationships. *Journal of Divorce & Remarriage, 49*(1–2), 78–109. https://doi.org/10.1080/10502550801973005

30 Smith-Etxeberria, K., & Eceiza, A. (2021). Mother–child and father–child relationships in emerging adults from divorced and non-divorced families. *Social Sciences, 10*(10), 382. https://doi.org/10.3390/socsci10100382

31 Kalmijn, M. (2015). Relationships between fathers and adult children: The cumulative effects of divorce and repartnering. *Journal of Family Issues, 36*(6), 737–759. https://doi.org/10.1177/0192513X13495398

32 van Schaick, K., & Stolberg, A. L. (2001). The impact of paternal involvement and parental divorce on young adults' intimate relationships. *Journal of Divorce & Remarriage, 36*(1–2), 99–121. https://doi.org/10.1300/J087v36n01_06

33 Ali, M. M., & Dean, D., Jr. (2015). The influence of nonresident fathers on adolescent and young adult cigarette smoking. *Families, Systems, & Health, 33*(3), 314–323. https://doi.org/10.1037/fsh0000137

# 9

# Conclusion

## Relationships Matter and Lessons from Development

*[Fathers] are the single greatest untapped resource in the lives of American children.*[1]
—Kyle D. Pruett, Yale Medical School

In this final chapter, we offer conclusions about fathering based on the growing body of fatherhood research and practice. *Fathers and Children Together* is different from most popular literature in that we relied on research on fathers and the authors' practice experiences to answer questions that fathers frequently ask about parenting. We want to make one thing clear: research and practice by themselves do not drive the changing culture of fatherhood. Fathers and mothers are responsible for the trends in fathering behavior at the family level. The growing trend for increased father involvement with children is the consequence of fathers' own desires to be closer and more involved with their children. Mothers and others are also expecting and encouraging fathers to be actively engaged with children. Mothers have entered and stayed in the labor force in large numbers throughout the United States and in other parts of the world. Fatherhood research shines a light on important areas of fathers' influence on children's development and potential areas for fathers' personal growth and development. Practice with fathers provides insight into information and educational practices that help fathers to

DOI: 10.4324/9781003486107-9

develop their reflective capacity and parenting skills. Fathers have had to become involved caregivers. In the process of becoming more involved with children, many fathers have discovered the joys and challenges of raising children. They have found joy in watching children grow and develop. Many fathers talk about feeling intense love for their children and how much love their children have for them.[2] They have also come to appreciate the greater sense of purpose that goes along with becoming a father. Fathers have also discovered that caring for children can be one of the hardest jobs a person can have. Countless fathers have told us that they were not prepared to be a parent and that parenting is harder than any job they have held outside of the home.

This chapter summarizes the main themes and insights that surface from reviewing the developmental journey of *fathers and children together* from prenatal through young adult development. We revisit the concept of father identity that emerges during the prenatal period and the initial reflections on values that fathers want to pass on to their young children. The ecological and family systems contexts are important for understanding the diversity of ways that men choose to engage in fatherhood. Fathers learn alongside their children and adapt and grow to keep up with the rapid pace of their child's development. One of the consistent themes across developmental stages has been the importance of fathers in providing emotional security to their developing children. Fathers' own development and the benefits that come from embracing involved fatherhood are also important themes. Our experiences as researchers and practitioners who are involved with developing and evaluating programs for fathers have convinced us of the importance of creating more programs to support fathers and families.

Fathers' growth and development begins with building an identity as a father before their child is born. The extent to which fathers are engaged with their children greatly influences the integration of fatherhood into men's identity. For fathers who are involved with their children, building this new identity includes constructing a new configuration of roles. Fathers need to decide how their new role as a parent fits with their other roles, which may include husband, partner, employee, friend, brother, and son. In the prenatal chapter, we wrote that the integration of these social roles into a new identity is a challenging developmental task. Men value their role as involved fathers. Many fathers value their roles as nurturers and protectors as more important than their provider role.[3] There is possibly no role that is more important than being an "involved dad."

Throughout the book, the authors include questions for reflection on important values to pass on to children and how these influence parenting practices. Fathers have the privilege and responsibility to raise their children to be good people and productive citizens. They also have the right to select the values that they want to encourage in their children. Glen, as a parent educator, has emphasized that his role is not to instruct parents on the "right way" to raise children. First, there is no right way for all children and, second, parents get to choose the values and goals they have for their children. The parent educator role helps fathers understand their values and decide which parenting practices best fit with their goals. Careful reflection on one's values helps fathers to be more thoughtful, intentional, understanding, and consistent. There are many right ways to parent that can lead to positive outcomes for children and close father–child relationships. Reflection on both values and parenting practices can help men to become better fathers. We trust that some of our questions for reflection have helped guide more thoughtful parenting practices that support positive father–child relationships.

We have seen throughout this book that the context of fathers' lives matters. We have used the ecological-systems model to explain that there are multiple influences on fathers and children. These influences include neighborhoods, schools, community and health care resources, social media, economic security, and social policies. Culture plays an important role in how fathers raise their children. For example, Black fathers engage in racial socialization because their children are often exposed to negative stereotypes. Jewish and Muslim fathers frequently teach their children about antisemitism or anti-Muslim hatred. Talking with children prepares them to deal with discrimination and to develop a healthy identity.

One of the most important contextual factors is the family. We have used family systems theory to explain the importance of family relationships to positive fathering and child development. Fathering takes place in the context of fathers' and mothers' relationships with their own parents, other children in the family (if any), the quality of family communication, and a multitude of family stresses and resources. Most importantly, fathering takes place in the context of father–mother coparenting relationships. We have seen that throughout child development, the support that fathers and mothers give each other, their ability to manage conflict, and the extent to which they share the responsibilities of parenting has a great influence on father–child relationships.

A growing number of men do not live with their children. Most nonresident fathers continue to be involved with their children and to coparent with the mother. Jay and his colleagues have suggested that the quality of the coparenting relationship may be even more important in these families where fathers and children live apart.[4] When the coparenting relationship breaks down, nonresident fathers face greater challenges in maintaining a relationship with children. Some mothers restrict nonresident fathers' access to children and avoid coparenting with them when there is a high level of conflict between parents or when parents have new intimate partners. Nonresident fathers may need the assistance of professional counselors or lawyers when they are unable to resolve differences with mothers about contact with children.

The ecological-systems model also indicates that fathers' personalities and belief systems influence how they parent their children. In the introductory chapter, we identified masculinity as an important principle for understanding fatherhood—how men define masculinity impacts how they see their role as fathers. Some men have traditional ideals about being a man and tend to believe that their main role is to provide financially for the family. Other men have less traditional ideals about masculinity and tend to believe that they should be highly involved in caring for children. Ideals about masculinity are socially constructed by men and women. One thing is clear: beliefs about masculinity impact how men assume the father role. Many men have

changed their beliefs about masculinity and adopted a more rela-
tion-focused perspective on masculinity through being with and
nurturing their children on a daily basis. These belief changes
have led men to value relational skills and caring in new ways.

We wrote in the introductory chapter that fathers must grow
and adapt as children grow and develop. Children's growth and
development signals a need for fathers to change. For example,
when children grow from infants to active toddlers, fathers must
learn to assist and protect children as they begin to actively
explore their environment. Interacting with toddlers and keeping
them safe day after day can be exhausting. Many fathers report
great joy in watching their children grow and develop, but they
also report that adapting to children's needs can be challenging.
They may not have realized how much close supervision and
constant care toddlers require. Fathers may have to better manage their own activities (e.g., cell phone use) and emotions (e.g.,
managing toddler meltdowns) to adapt to the changing needs of
their toddlers. Fathers also learn that adapting caregiving and
limit-setting practices to the needs of children is a continual process. They may adapt to the changes from infancy to toddlerhood
only to find out that there are new changes to be made with preschoolers, who have boundless energy and are full of questions
about everything.

We hope that we have helped fathers to realize their importance in raising healthy, well-adjusted children. Fathers can
have important positive effects on children during every stage
of development, from before the child's birth through emerging
adulthood. During each stage of development, fathers who are
sensitive and attuned to their children's needs help their children
to become healthy, well-adjusted individuals and develop the
skills needed to express and understand emotions, understand
the world around them, and interact with others in a socially
competent manner. However, the influences that fathers have
on children continue to change as children mature and grow
older. For example, during middle childhood, children need
their fathers to help with homework assignments, to support
their interests, and to assist in teaching responsibility through
household chores. Although fathers also help their adolescents

with these tasks, most adolescents become more independent and need less supervision and assistance from fathers.

Even so, adolescence brings on new tasks for fathers. Fathers must find a balance between supporting children's strivings for independence and ensuring their adolescents are safe and behave responsibly. Fathers must also support their adolescent's efforts to explore and construct their identity. In emerging adulthood, fathers support their children by helping them to find direction in life, supporting their continuing education, and encouraging their financial independence. As children's developmental tasks change, fathers must learn how to understand and support their children's needs and interests.

There is one area of fathering behavior that emerges as a critical constant, and that is fathers' provision of emotional security to their children. Through every stage of development, fathers are needed to provide support and respond to their children's needs for security. This does not mean that fathers should accept all their children's behaviors. There are many times when fathers need to communicate their expectations that children should behave differently. We have stated throughout this book that fathers are most effective when they use authoritative parenting styles rather than authoritarian or permissive parenting styles. Fathers who communicate expectations for behavior in a supportive manner are more effective in helping children to be cooperative than fathers who demand obedience. We have referred to attachment theory and Circle of Security as a model throughout this book to suggest how fathers can be a secure base for children to explore the world as they become more independent as well as being a safe haven to provide emotional support when their children need comfort and security. The Circle of Security model encourages fathers to be confident leaders and balances being kind without becoming weak and being strong without becoming mean.[5] The Circle of Security model is applicable to fathers at every stage of child development.

The research evidence is clear that men who are involved in their children's lives also benefit, including their own social and emotional development. Daniel Singley and Lisa Edwards have written that positive parenting makes men less self-centered and more focused on others.[6] Singley and Edwards state that fathers acquire a capacity for love and a sense of optimism about humanity when they respond appropriately to the changing needs of children. They learn flexibility. They learn that there are limits to what parents can do to shape their children's outcomes, because children have their own motivations and personalities. Being with children, especially during the early years, can promote father's psychological growth and development in the following ways:

◆ Delayed gratification of one's own needs
◆ New opportunities for learning empathy
◆ New levels of emotional intensity and regulation
◆ Increased levels of self-awareness and self-scrutiny
◆ Expanded understanding of nurturance and care

Fathers who are involved also experience a greater sense of purpose and well-being. Men who embrace fatherhood as an important responsibility also may benefit from a decrease in negative behaviors, such as fewer accidents, less drug abuse, and less contact with the criminal justice system. Men are most likely to reap the benefits of involved fatherhood when the following conditions exist:[7]

◆ Commitment and motivation to be an involved father
◆ Significant amount and quality of involvement
◆ Energy and time to devote to parenting role
◆ A commitment to learning that supports questioning and reflecting on parent experiences

We have written throughout this book that fathers often lack supports for becoming involved fathers. At every stage of child development, fathers indicate that they could use more support and better role models for parenting. They often are not sure where to turn to when they need support for parenting. In the prenatal chapter, we saw that many expectant fathers do not know what is expected of them during the pregnancy. They feel excluded in their contacts with professionals and would like support to manage their own anxieties and understand the challenges and rewards of becoming an involved father. In the chapters on infancy, we saw that fathers often want to better understand how to support mothers' breastfeeding and how to care for newborns because they have not learned these skills during their own upbringing. We saw that nonresident fathers need support to maintain close relationships with children when those around them are not encouraging their involvement, which may lead them to withdraw from parenting responsibilities.

There are a growing number of community supports for fathers, but there is a great need for more. While some programs have been developed for fathers over the past four decades, they are not readily available or accessible. Our society has increased expectations for men to be involved fathers, but we have generally left men to figure out how to do this on their own. Many fathers manage this with the support of their partners. We have also experienced the power of programs to support the potential growth and development of men into the involved fathers that Kyle Pruett, quoted at the beginning of this chapter, imagined in 2000 would not only benefit children and families but help build stronger communities[8]. Health care, social service, education, and justice institutions can do more to engage fathers and to communicate an expectation that parenting is not something that one does alone. All parents deserve and can benefit from parenting education and support. As the expression goes, it takes a village to raise a child.

In conclusion, Jay and Glen want to say, "there is no one size fits all" when it comes to fathering. There is no universal standard for how involved fathers should be. Some fathers share parenting equally with mothers. In other families, fathers take on most of the breadwinning responsibilities while mothers may stay home with children or work part-time. In all these families, fathers are more involved with children than they were 50 years ago. There are also fathers who stay home with their young children while their mother works full-time. In many families, both fathers and mothers work full-time or nearly full-time, but mothers still assume more childcare responsibilities than fathers. Mothers have sometimes found it easier to assume more responsibility for childcare rather than pressure fathers to do more, even though they would like fathers to be more involved. It is easy for fathers and mothers to fall unintentionally into traditional gendered patterns of family responsibilities. Complicating matters are different perceptions of shared parenting. Mothers often say they are taking on more childcare responsibilities than fathers, while fathers say that childcare is shared equally.[9] We do not fault fathers and mothers for slipping into or choosing these patterns of parenting. Family life is challenging and parents have to balance childrearing responsibilities in ways that work best for their families. No matter what type of parenting roles fathers and mothers have assumed, fathers are more involved in caring for children today than they were in past decades. Fathers have more opportunities through involved fathering to influence their children's development and enhance their own adult development.

A great deal has been learned about fathers and children during the past several decades. Fifty years ago, there was barely any research that included fathers, and there were virtually no programs for fathers. Since that time, researchers and practitioners have learned a great deal about fathers and the ways in which they contribute to their children's development as well as their own development. We wrote this book because we believe that fathers, mothers, practitioners, students, and others deserve to know about this growing knowledge. We also believe that fathers deserve more than a simplified advice book about positive parenting. Raising and caring for children is perhaps the most significant role that a man can occupy. Many fathers express the desire to become more knowledgeable about how to be a good father. We hope this book provides this knowledge and affirms the importance of involved fathers to guide children's development, build stable family systems, and healthy communities.

## Notes

1  Pruett, K. D. (2000). *Fatherneed: Why father care is as essential as mother care for your child.* Free Press.
2  Mahalik, J. R., Di Bianca, M., & Sepulveda, J. A. (2020). Examining father status and purpose to understand new dads' healthier lives. *Psychology of Men & Masculinities, 21*(4), 570–577. https://doi.org/10.1037/men0000256

3 Minnesota Fathers and Families Network. (2007). *Do we count fathers in Minnesota: Searching for key indicators of the well-being of fathers and families.* Author.

4 Fagan, J., & Palkovitz, R. (2019). Coparenting and father engagement among low-income parents: Actor–partner interdependence model. *Journal of Family Psychology, 33,* 894–904. http://dx.doi.org/10.1037/fam0000563

5 Powell, B., Cooper, G., Hoffman, K., & Marvin, B. (2014). *The Circle of Security intervention: Enhancing attachment in early parent–child relationships.* Guilford Press.

6 Singley, D. B., & Edwards, L. M. (2015). Men's perinatal mental health in transition to fatherhood. *Professional Psychology: Research and Practice, 46*(5), 309–316. https://doi.org/10.1037/pro0000032

7 Palkovitz, R. (2002). *Involved fathering and men's adult development.* Lawrence Erlbaum Associates; Palm, G. F. (1993). Involved fatherhood: A second chance. *The Journal of Men's Studies, 2*(2), 139–155.

8 Pruett, K. D. (2000). *Fatherneed.*

9 Shaeffer, K. (2020). *Working moms in the U.S. have faced challenges on multiple fronts during the pandemic.* Pew Research Center. https://www.pewresearch.org/short-reads/2022/05/06/working-moms-in-the-u-s-have-faced-challenges-on-multiple-fronts-during-the-pandemic/

# Index

Printed in the United States
by Baker & Taylor Publisher Services